CONTENTS

1 The Neoclassical Parliament building was designed by the Danish architect Theophil Hansen. Its pediment is adorned with statues depicting Franz Joseph granting the Constitution to the 17 provinces of the Austro-Hungarian Empire.

2-7 This painting of the Schloss Hof shows the building silhouetted against an immense sky, in the typical style of the artist Bernardo Bellotto, nephew of Canaletto (Giovanni Antonio Canal) by whose name he is known in Austria.

3-6 The Upper Belvedere was built just southeast of the city center by Johann Lucas von Hildebrandt (1668-1745) for Prince Eugene of Savoy. The complex is one of the most harmonious examples of Baroque architecture.

VIENNA

PLACES AND HISTORY

Text by Elisabetta Canoro
Photographs by Marcello Libra

Graphic design
Maria Cucchi

© 2008 White Star S.p.A.
Via Candido Sassone, 22/24
13100 Vercelli, Italy
www.whitestar.it

TRANSLATION:
SARAH PONTING

ISBN 978-88-544-0373-4

RISTAMPE:
1 2 3 4 5 6   12 11 10 09 08

Color separation Grafotitoli, Milan
Printed in Indonesia

8 top left Schönbrunn Palace reflects the feminine taste of Maria Theresa, who personally chose the architect Nikolaus Pacassi to design it. The empress oversaw all aspects of the project and the progress of the work, which commenced in 1746 and was completed three years later, albeit with successive additions and remodeling.

8 top right Built in eclectic style between 1881 and 1914, the Neue Burg was the last wing to be added to the Hofburg. It is characterized by a crescent-shaped façade with an colonnade overlooking the Heldenplatz ("Heroes Square"), which is dominated by an equestrian monument of Prince Eugene of Savoy.

8-9 On fine summer days the view from St. Stephen's Cathedral alone is worth a visit to the Austrian capital. This Gothic masterpiece was initially built as a Romanesque church in the 13th century. However, the original edifice was destroyed in a fire and it was rebuilt in its present form between the 14th and 16th centuries.

9 The Baroque Pestsäule ("Plague Column"), on the Graben, is a tribute to the return to normal life, for it commemorates the end of the terrible plague epidemic that struck Europe in 1679.

I n 2001 UNESCO inscribed the historic center of Vienna on its World Heritage List for the following reasons: its urban and architectural qualities bear outstanding witness to a continuing interchange of values throughout the second millennium; it clearly illustrates three key periods of European cultural and political development – the Middle Ages, the Baroque period, and the Gründerzeit (the "Founding Epoch," roughly corresponding to the final quarter of the 19th century); and for centuries it has been universally acknowledged as the musical capital of Europe.

The acknowledgment paid to the Habsburg capital by the prestigious international organization – which in 1996 had already inscribed the magnificent Palace and Gardens of Schönbrunn on its List – endorses a unique historical district that developed in the Innere Stadt (Inner City) and along the monumental Ringstrasse (Ring Street). A frontier city and a natural meeting point of East and West, the Austrian capital is the product of the many cultures of the huge area that was once subject to the rule of the Habsburg monarchs. The Austrian dynasty wore the crown of Holy Roman Emperor almost uninterruptedly between 1438 and 1806, at its height determining the destiny of half the world. Emperor Charles V – upon whose empire the sun never set – was the result of the shrewd marriage policy commenced by Emperor Frederick III, which characterized the family's strategy over the centuries. Indeed, Empress Maria Theresa arranged lucrative marriages for most of her 16 children, earning herself the nickname of the "mother-in-law of Europe!"

The supranational empire of Christendom was broken by Napoleonic expansion, however, and Francis Joseph's Austro-Hungarian Empire dissolved after its defeat in World War I. Although Vienna always played the role of a prestigious international court, the pivotal location that underlay its success also made it the object of many attacks and sieges, from both East and West. It was violated by Bohemian and Hungarian kings, the troops of the Grand Vizier and by Napoleon's armies. But it was the Ottomans who were the city's greatest bane, and Vienna remained suppressed and paralyzed in the shadow of the Gothic bell tower of the cathedral, guarded by a "little" Hofburg (Court City), awaiting a time in which it could burgeon. This came after the Turks had been definitively driven back in 1683, and Vienna

became a bustling construction site under Leopold I and subsequently Charles VI and Maria Theresa.

The Baroque style associated with the presence at court of a large number of Italian families of architects, sculptors, decorators and painters merged with an Austrian one championed by Johann Fischer von Erlach and his son Joseph Emanuel and Johann Lukas von Hildebrandt. The three architects competed with each other, remodeling churches and building palaces for the aristocracy and emperors (including the

Belvedere and Schönbrunn), giving the city the architecture that now characterizes it at least as much as the spectacular Ringstrasse – opened in 1857 by Francis Joseph – on which the middle class built their eclectic "temples."

The arrival of Gluck and Salieri at court marked the beginning of the Wiener Klassik (Vienna Classical), a particularly fertile period for musical composition, which reached its height with Haydn and Mozart. Vienna was a magnet for and the cradle of many legendary figures of classical music and opera, and

Beethoven, Schubert, Brahms, Léhar, Schönberg and Webern composed their masterpieces on the banks of the "beautiful Blue Danube" celebrated by Strauss – a sort of second national anthem – from the late 1700s to the first half of the 20th century.

The Strauss family, and particularly the prolific Johann Sebastian, inaugurated the golden season of waltzes and court balls, which today still mark the society debuts of the young scions of the nobility.

The Viennese have a deep passion for the magical world of music, decreeing the

success or failure of operas and operettas, crowding theaters with programs capable of exhausting even the most relentless music lovers, and rightly taking pride in their orchestra, the Vienna Philharmonic – the most famous in the world – whose New Year Concerts are televised worldwide each year.

The city bears the traces of all of these aspects, sometimes hidden among the folds of its sumptuous and somewhat pompous palaces. Vienna is at once an artistic and cultural laboratory – think, for example, of Stefan Zweig, Robert Musil, Joseph Roth, Karl Kraus, Arthur Schnitzler and Sigmund Freud – a collection of platitudes, and a myriad of astonishing surprises.

The "Habsburg myth," which took shape following the disappearance of the powerful dynasty, has contributed to the image of a sleeping beauty incapable of "sullying herself" by incorporating "foreign bodies" in her regal and closely woven fabric. However, this is not the case. Indeed, the city has – sometimes reluctantly – absorbed many new buildings, such as the Looshaus, by Adolf Loos (1870-1933), built in 1911 opposite the Imperial Palace. The architectural and pictorial adventures of the Secessionists, the huge housing projects of "Red Vienna" built between the two world wars, the curved lines and bright colors with which Friedensreich Hundertwasser embodied his extraordinary dream of happiness and beauty, the "deconstructionist roofs" that rise airily on the skyline, like those of Coop Himmelblau on Falkestrasse, and Hans Hollein's icy steel and glass constructions have all become symbols of the city.

With its 23 districts and almost 2 million inhabitants, in recent decades Vienna has

once again become a cosmopolitan and buzzing metropolis, in which past and future merge with masterly results.

This revival is symbolized by the MuseumsQuartier, one of the largest museum complexes in the world, in which futuristic "cubes" are grafted onto the Baroque structure of the 17th-century imperial mews in the city center. In short, the city has become a contemporary international capital, whose intimate and welcoming side can still be seen in its historic cafés and carefully manicured gardens.

FROM ROMAN VINDOBONA TO THE THIRD UNO CENTER

20 top The title of Holy Roman Emperor can be traced back to Charlemagne (742-814), depicted here by Albrecht Dürer. The title subsequently passed to Germany, and then to Austria in the 15th century.

Although Vienna's fame and "personality" are bound up with the epic of the dynasty that dominated Europe for over 6 centuries, its history commenced 2000 years ago with the arrival of the Romans in Pannonia, when 6000 of Emperor Marcus Aurelius' legionaries settled a site already inhabited by Celts. Vindobona was not merely a fortified post, but a permanent military camp whose asymmetrical layout followed the conformation of the land and the river. It was from this camp – and not from the civilian settlement that grew up alongside it – that the modern city center developed, as testified by the finds in the Hoher Markt.

The intense "traffic" of barbarian peoples that followed the fall of the Roman Empire continued until Charlemagne conquered the area.

The region was known as the Ostmark, or *marchia Orientalis*, which later became Ostarrîchi under the Holy Roman Emperor Otto III (reigned 936-973), from which Österreich, Austria's modern German name, is clearly derived.

In 976 the region was given to the house of Babenberg, whose head was appointed margrave – a title of the Holy Roman Empire given to the Germanic feudatories with jurisdiction over the border areas.

During their rule Vienna was made capital for the first time by Henry II Jasomirgott (1142), who erected a castle (of which no trace remains) in Am Hof square. The massive St Stephen's Cathedral was built on the ashes of the Romanesque church of the same name, consecrated in 1147 and destroyed by a fire in the following century.

Vienna was a thriving river port and thus a wealthy trading center, but it was also an important muster point for the armies departing and returning from the Crusades. Indeed, it was on his return from the Holy Land that Richard the Lion-Heart, king of England, was imprisoned (1192) after having refused to pay homage to the Babenberg flag. The ransom paid for his release financed the construction of the city's inner circle of walls, which was completed in 1200 and survived until 1857.

The presence of the first Jew in the city is also said to date from this episode. His name was Schlomo, as revealed by an official document from 1194, and he was summoned by Leopold V to transform the English silver into coins. The mint was built near the ducal palace and constituted the nucleus from which the old Jewish quarter developed, in the modern Judenplatz. Razed by the *Wiener Geserah* (Vienna Pogrom) in 1421, the ghetto was not rebuilt until 1625 in Leopoldstadt, between the Danube Canal and the river, but the Jews were once again expelled in 1670.

In 1221 Duke Leopold VI established Vienna's civic government, including the position of burgomaster. But 25 years later, in 1246, the Babenberg dynasty ended when Frederick II was slain in battle.

20 bottom Leopold VI, the Glorious (1489-92), of the house of Babenberg, Duke of Austria from 1198 to 1230, depicted in a detail of a triptych by Hans Part, in Klosterneubeurg Monastery as he reconciles the Holy Roman Emperor Frederick II with the pope by means of the Treaty of San Germano (1230).

21 This detail of a triptych by Hans Part, painted during the 15th century and housed in Klosterneubeurg Monastery, shows Adalbert of Babenberg fighting the Hungarians.

VIENNA PANNONIE

During the following 30 years, the Austrian territory passed to Ottakar II, king of Bohemia and pretender to the Imperial throne. He started to build the new church of St Stephen, whose traces can still be seen in the cathedral façade, and a castle, from which the great Hofburg subsequently developed. However, Rudolf I of Habsburg, elected emperor of the Holy Roman Empire in 1273, seized Ottokar's crown and city. The conqueror remained in Vienna for a while, winning the approval of the local aristocracy, and in 1282 he invested his son Albert with the Duchy of Austria. Following Albert's election as emperor in 1298, with the title Albert I, he started to rebuild the cathedral in Gothic style, starting with the choir (1304). However, his murder in 1308 and the ensuing vendetta of his sons generated much resentment toward the Habsburgs, who were not re-elected emperors for over 100 years.

Rudolf IV of Austria was highly ambitious, as demonstrated by his forgery of the *Privilegium Maius*, which served to increase his power. In 1359, he laid the first stone of the Steffl (as the Viennese affectionately call St Stephen's Cathederal), and founded the University on March 12, 1365 with the clear intention of ensuring that his name would be remembered. Following the election of Albert II as emperor in 1438, the title remained in the hands of the Habsburgs until Napoleon dissolved the Holy Roman Empire in 1806. Albert's successor, Frederick III (1415-93), raised Austria to an archduchy and commenced the shrewd marriage policy that expanded his house's territories as far as South America. His son Maximilian, who ruled as Emperor Maximilian I from

1493 to 1519 and who founded of the Vienna Boys' Choir (1498), married Mary of Burgundy when he was just 18 years old. Their sole male heir was Philip, father of Charles V (whose mother was Joanna the Mad, daughter of Isabella of Castile), who ruled over a vast empire from Madrid. Ferdinand, entrusted by his brother Charles with the government of Austria, was forced to deal with the Turks, who were clamoring at the gates of the Catholic West.

24 top Maximilian II (1527-76), Emperor of the Holy Roman Empire and King of Bohemia and Hungary, whose portrait can be admired at the Musée du Château de Versailles.

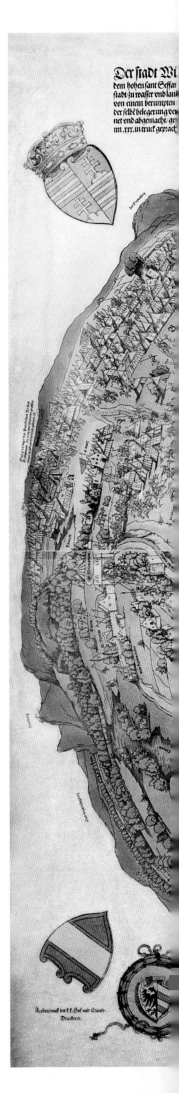

Already damaged by a terrible fire, in 1529 Vienna was besieged for 18 days by the armies of Suleiman the Magnificent, and was saved only by the early arrival of winter. Following his accession to the imperial throne in 1556, Ferdinand I rebuilt the city walls in the style of an Italian fortress and made the capital a prestigious international court.

When Ferdinand's successor Maximilian II (1527-76) – founder of the famous Spanish Riding School – granted freedom of worship, 80 percent of the city's population declared itself Protestant. Commissioned by the many religious orders that arrived in the early 17th century, families of architects and artists, such as the Carlone, Canevale, Tencalla, Martinelli, Rossi and Galli da Bibiena, built and remodeled Vienna's churches (particularly in the maze of medieval streets behind the cathedral) bringing the forms of the Roman Baroque to the city. The Jesuitenkirche (1627-31), redecorated by Andrea Pozzo in 1703-05, rises above them all. During this period the Thirty Years War (1618-48) was raging throughout Europe.

24 bottom This gouache on paper of the Ottoman school, from the Hunername by Lokman, housed in the Topkapi Palace Museum in Istanbul, shows Suleiman the Magnificent besieging the Austrian capital.

24-25 A 19th-century color lithograph of an original woodcut by Nikolaus Meldemann depicts the first siege of Vienna by the Turks led by Suleiman in 1529.

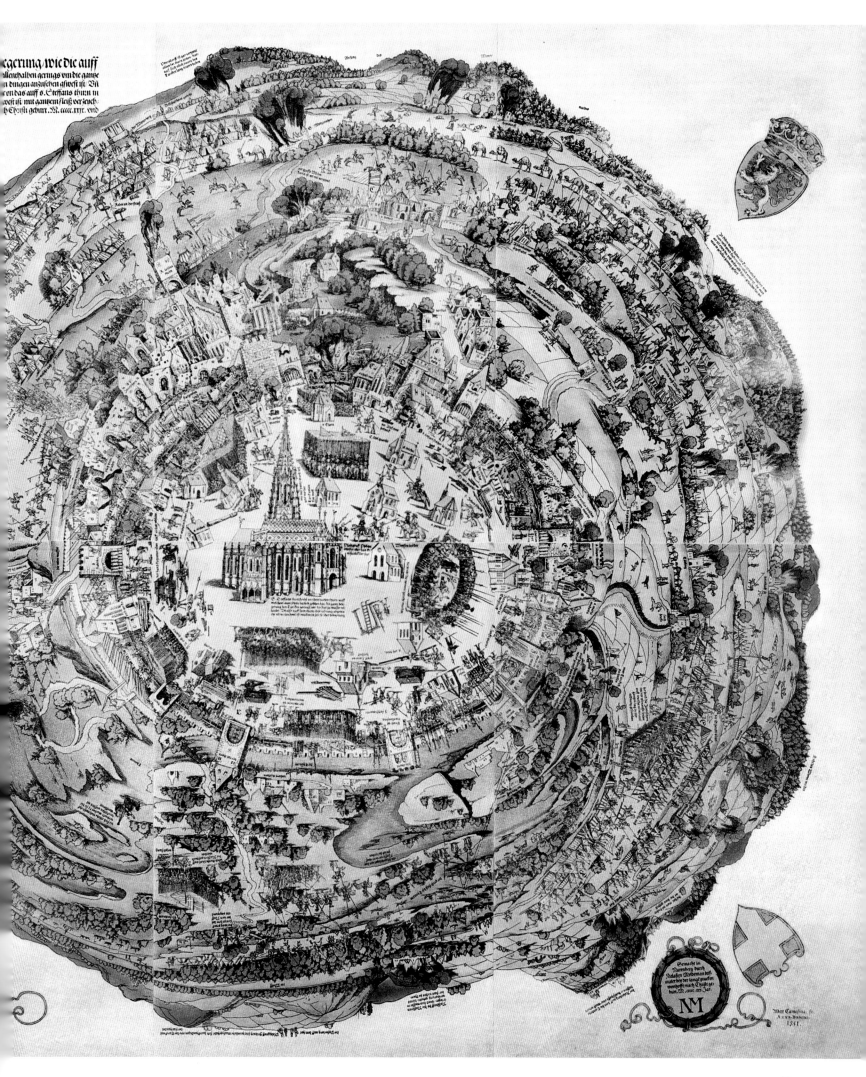

26 *A portrait in the Wien Museum Karlsplatz shows the Grand Vizier Kara Mustafa (1634-83), who led the 100,000-man Ottoman army.*

26-27 *This 17th-century painting shows the second Turkish siege of Vienna, which commenced on July 14, 1683, and ended on September 12th of the same year, when the John III Sobieski defeated the invading army at the command of Polish,* *Austrian and German troops.*

27 top *This 17th-century Turkish map, housed in the Wien Museum Karlsplatz, shows the city at the time of the 1683 siege, which was the second and last attempted by the Ottoman army.*

The end of the war did not, unfortunately, mark the end of the city's troubles. In 1679, following the ascent to the throne of Emperor Leopold I (1640-1705), 30,000 people died in a plague epidemic, and four years later the Turks, this time led by the grand vizier Kara Mustafa, again besieged Vienna.

However, the exhausted city managed to resist for a couple of months until the arrival of the Polish king John III Sobieski

Chara Musta:
Anno 1683 den 12
aber wider den 12
Spott Dheck geschlagen

Tha Türckischer Groß Vezier welcher
Zülÿ die Kaÿ: Residenz Staft Wien Belagert
Er: mit verlust vnd großen
Worden

with a relieving army. Vienna "inherited" the bronze cannons left behind by the retreating Ottomans, which were used to cast the Pummerin bell in St Stephen's Cathedral, and their sacks of coffee beans, which gave rise to the fashion of the Viennese cafés that were destined to become a mainstay of the city's social and cultural life.

Some also claim that croissants are another reminder of this event and were invented by bakers who celebrated the victory with a crescent-shaped pastry. The definitive defeat of the Turks marked the start of a long period of peace for the city (although not for the rest of Europe, where the Habsburgs were desperately struggling to defend imperial territory). As a precaution, during the War of the Spanish Succession with the French, Leopold I built a second ring of walls around the city, thus enclosing the suburbs that had developed around historic center.

Baroque buildings appeared all over the city, designed chiefly by Johann Bernard and Joseph Emanuel Fischer von Erlach, and Johann Lukas von Hildebrandt, who continued to employ talented Italian artists for the decoration of their interiors. Between political engagements, Leopold I – a dedicated music lover – summoned great composers and librettists, including Nicolò Minato and Antonio Draghi, to the imperial court.

When the city was struck by yet another plague epidemic in 1713, Emperor Charles VI vowed to build a great church dedicated to St Charles Borromeo, protector of plague victims. The commission was granted to Johann Bernard Fischer von Erlach, who built Vienna's finest Baroque church, inspired by the classical architecture of ancient Greece and Rome. The Milanese saint's statue was placed in the tympanum of the pediment and episodes of his life are depicted in the reliefs of the two columns, modeled on that of Trajan in Rome.

Destined for the imperial throne following her father's promulgation of the Pragmatic Sanction, which allowed succession to the Habsburg monarchy regardless of sex, Maria Theresa nonetheless had to fight for her title. In 1745 she managed to get her husband Francis Stephen of Lorraine elected as emperor. However, it was actually Maria Theresa who dealt with political matters, allowing her consort plenty of free time to dedicate to his real passion of natural history. The empress, who ruled until 1780, embraced the ideas of enlightened absolutism, developing and centralizing government, reforming the legal, educational and health systems, boosting the economy with the creation of new factories, and constructing important roads. Her son Joseph II (1780-90) followed in his mother's footsteps and is remembered as the "revolutionary emperor," for he guaranteed religious freedom, abolished serfdom, replaced Latin with German in official documents and confiscated the properties of the Church. This was decidedly too much for the conservative aristocracy, which forced him to withdraw some of his reforms. During the ten years of his rule he surrounded himself with philosophers and men of letters and promoted music and the arts.

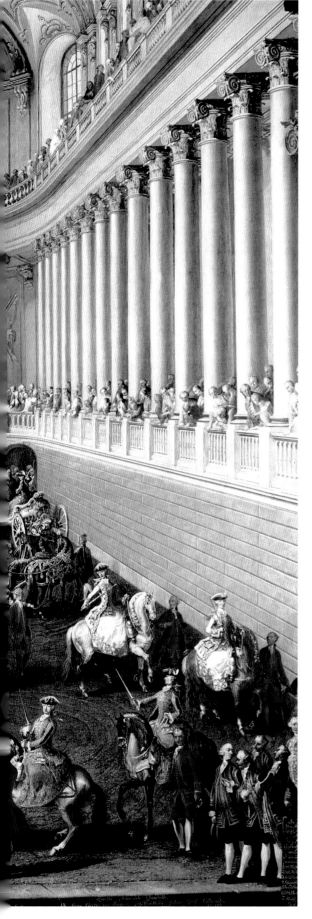

At the same time that Mozart arrived in Vienna (his first performance at court was during the rule of Maria Teresa, when he gave a concert at the Schönbrunn palace at the age of just six years old, winning the heart of the empress), the libertine Lorenzo Da Ponte, became court librettist to Joseph II on the recommendation of Antonio Salieri. During his appointment Da Ponte wrote the libretti for Mozart's most important operas, from *Le nozze di Figaro* (1786) to *Don Giovanni* (1787) and *Così fan tutte* (1790). Mozart struck up a friendship with the old Joseph Haydn, who had commenced his career in the Vienna Boys' Choir and ended up as the teacher of Beethoven and Schubert.

30-31 Empress Maria Theresa leads the mounted parade held on January 2, 1743, following the withdrawal of the Franco-Bavarian army from Bohemia, in a painting by Martin van Meytens (1695-1770).

31 top This engraving from the Wien Museum is the title page of a piano concerto by Wolfgang Amadeus Mozart (1756-91), the celebrated Austrian composer who produced his greatest works in Vienna, where he started to compose and perform while still a child.

31 bottom An oil painting by Martin van Meytens (1695-1770), now housed in Schönbrunn Palace, shows Mozart as a child, performing at the banquet held for the wedding of Joseph II and Isabella of Parma, which took place on October 6, 1760 in Vienna.

In 1792 conservative Europe found itself facing revolutionary France and the grand designs of Napoleon, who twice occupied Vienna (in 1805 and 1809), marking the end of the supranational empire of Christendom founded by Charlemagne. In 1806, Napoleon dissolved the Holy Roman Empire, and the Holy Roman Emperor Francis II became Emperor of Austria with the name Francis I.

A key figure at the Congress of Vienna, held in 1814-15 following Napoleon's first abdication, was Prince Klemens Wenzel von Metternich, who went on to head the Austrian government. Under Metternich Vienna recovered a little of its lost prestige, in part because of the emergence of a burgeoning middle class. In the field of art, the need for domestic intimacy and tranquil comfort were encapsulated – particularly in interior decoration – in the Biedermeier style, which was the antithesis of the pompous Empire style. This particular period is also – and perhaps more correctly – known as the Pre-March period, referring to the revolutionary wave that ravaged Europe in 1848. Indeed, Austria's political and economic recovery had been accompanied by a sharp reversal in terms of freedom, for Metternich had suppressed civil rights and the country had found itself at the mercy of a police regime.

34 This watercolor
by an unknown artist
shows a demonstration
at the entrance to a
Viennese factory in
1848.

34-35 This delicate
illustration
commemorates the
wedding of Franz Joseph
(1830-1916) and
Elisabeth (1837-98).

35 A period
photograph of a
painting by Georg
Decker, dating from
around 1881 and
depicting the

Emperor Franz
Joseph with his
beautiful but
unhappy wife,
familiarly known as
Sisi, and their family.

On March 13, 1848 the army opened fire
on demonstrators who had gathered in front
of the Landhaus to demand reform, triggering
a general uprising. After months of cruel
struggle the Viennese surrendered, but
Metternich was forced to resign and
Ferdinand I to abdicate.

On December 2, 1848 Francis Joseph I
ascended the throne. Serious, observant of
the rules, taciturn and reserved, rational and
completely unimaginative, "Franzl" ruled the
Austrian empire for 68 years, making him its
longest reigning monarch. The son of a mild-
mannered father (Archduke Francis Charles,
who ceded him the imperial title) and an
ironhanded mother (Princess Sophie of
Bavaria), Francis Joseph survived the
breakdown of the empire and a series of
family tragedies: his brother Maximilian I,
Emperor of Mexico, was executed by
Republican forces led by Benito Juárez
(1867); his only son, Rudolf, committed
suicide at the age of 30 with his young
mistress Baroness Mary Vetsera at his hunting
lodge in Mayerling (1889); and his beloved
wife Elisabeth von Wittelsbach – the restless
and unconventional Sisi who still occupies a
special place in the hearts of the Viennese

people – was assassinated in Geneva by the Italian anarchist Luigi Luccheni (1898). However, nothing distracted him from his public duties, to which he attended personally in even the tiniest details.

In order to perform these duties Francis Joseph set himself a military-like schedule, rising at 4 o'clock each morning and working for 14 hours. His sole pleasures were an occasional waltz and hunting. He also dedicated very little time to official lunches, and Elisabeth, who frequently fasted to preserve her much-envied figure, often did not even appear at the table. Her husband, on the other hand, wolfed down everything at an incredible speed, and when he put down his fork, marking the end of the meal (as required by court etiquette), his unfortunate table companions had eaten little or nothing. It is told that it was this habit that determined the success of the nearby Hotel Sacher, which became the refuge of hungry diplomats and noblemen. Francis Joseph, Emperor of Austria and King of Hungary, gave Vienna its current appearance. In 1857 he demolished the wall that enclosed the Innere Stadt, annexing to the city the eight districts comprised in the outer ring.

36 top This engraving of Vienna, made in 1823, offers a panoramic view of the city, with St. Stephen's Cathedral visible in the background.

36-37 This 1873 view of Vienna by Gustav Veith, now housed in the Wien Museum Karlsplatz, shows the city with the new buildings overlooking the Ringstrasse, which replaced the old bastions and fortifications, demolished after the March Revolution of 1848.

37 top This painting by Siegmund l'Allemand, now housed in Schönbrunn Palace in Vienna, depicts the sumptuous banquet held on occasion of the anniversary of the Military Order of Maria Theresa in 1861.

37 bottom Francis II (1768-1835), the last Holy Roman Emperor and the first hereditary Emperor of Austria, returning to Vienna after a trip to Paris in 1814. The work was painted by Peter Krafft and is housed in the Kunsthistorisches Museum in Vienna.

In 1893 the outer wall too was demolished and Otto Wagner won the competition announced to redesign the city. In this task the functionalist architect gave priority to practical aspects, designing four ring roads intersected by long thoroughfares that radiated outwards to the suburbs (the modern districts 10-22, which were incorporated in the metropolitan area in 1890). Between 1894 and 1901 he built the metropolitan railway system, complete with viaducts and some 30 stations, which were designed to fit in with their different urban surroundings. The turn of the 20th century was a fervent time in Vienna. The Secessionist movement, to which Richard Wagner himself initially belonged, contrasted with the academic eclecticism of official art and encapsulated contemporary European artistic currents. The Vienna Secession expressed itself in all artistic fields, and particularly in the painting of Klimt, Schiele and Kokoschka, who moved freely from Symbolism to Expressionism. Olbrich's Secession Building, the group's architectural manifesto, stands just a stone's throw from the eclectic palaces of the Ringstrasse, set apart by its dazzling gold dome.

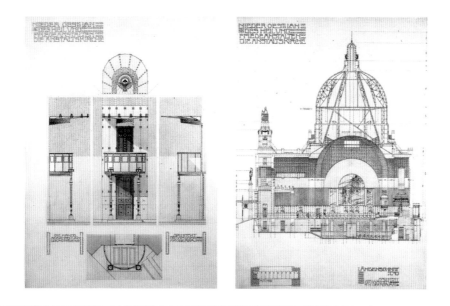

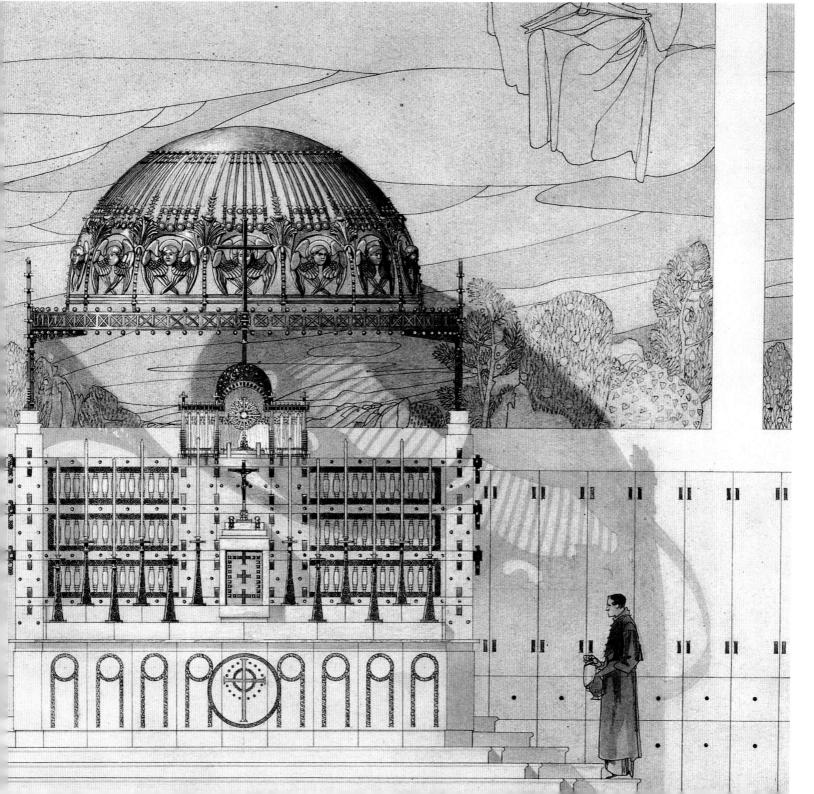

In 1914 the assassination of Archduke Francis Ferdinand, the heir to the throne, sparked World War II and the subsequent dissolution of the Austro-Hungarian Monarchy. Francis Joseph died in 1916 and was succeeded by Charles I, who in 1918 renounced all participation in affairs of state, but was nonetheless deposed by the Austrian parliament in 1919.

The empire, which had covered an area of 435,000 sq. miles (1,126,644 sq. km) with a population of 52 million people, no longer existed and Vienna became the overgrown capital of a republic reduced to 50,000 sq. miles (129,500 sq. km) with just 6 million inhabitants.

The economic crisis resulted in large-scale migration to the city, exacerbating the housing problem and posing an enormous challenge for the socialists, who won the elections held in 1919. The great housing projects built between 1919 and 1933 testify to this period that preceded the city's fall into the black hole of Nazism.

In 1933 Chancellor Engelbert Dollfuss (who was assassinated in 1934 for his hostility to Hitler's expansionist policy) abolished all political parties and established an authoritarian regime, seeking Mussolini's Italy as an ally. In 1938 the Reichstag (the German parliament) enacted the Anschluss (the Union): on March 15 Hitler triumphantly entered Vienna and announced the annexation of Austria to Germany to a cheering crowd in the Heldenplatz. At the end of World War II, the city – heavily bombed by the Allies – was divided into four sectors like Berlin. Its desolate atmosphere is evoked in Orson Welles' film *The Third Man* (1949).

40 bottom Two
small girls wander
among the rubble
in Vienna, which
suffered heavy
bombing during
World War II.

40-41 In 1945 a sign
marks the limit of the
area of Vienna under
American control, one
of the four quarters in
which the city was
divided.

42 A crowd cheers the politicians and diplomats on the balcony of the Belvedere palace on May 15, 1955, when the eagerly awaited treaty ending the Allied occupation of the city was signed.

42-43 Reconstruction and peace: in 1975, exactly 30 years after the catastrophic war, building was underway on the Vienna International Centre (also known as UNO City), a modern multipurpose complex with avant-garde architecture, whose extension is scheduled to be completed in 2012.

Vienna regained its freedom with the Austrian State Treaty signed at the Belvedere castle on May 15th, 1955, and its mayor, Theodor Körner, commenced a grand rebuilding program.

On October 26th of the same year Parliament drew up the Constitution establishing Austria's permanent neutrality, and the country became a member of the United Nations. In 1979 Vienna was chosen as the third headquarters of the United Nations, owing to its history, its pivotal location between East and West, and its new status as capital of a neutral state (and member of the European Union since 1995).

During the 1960s the city council started to extend the public transport network and embarked on several large-

scale projects, particularly in the public health sector. In 1966 the council approved modern plans for the construction of an underground railway network, and the first line was inaugurated in 1978. The metropolitan railway system was expanded, until connecting the north bank of the Danube with the southern outskirts of the city.

A rapid line, cutting the city from east to west, was also inaugurated. Investments in the public health sector allowed the construction of the Allgemeines Krankenhaus (General Hospital) and, during the 1990s, the "Medical Center East" in the neighborhoods north of the Danube. Parallel to the urban development projects, many schemes were launched to restore the city's architectural heritage.

THE INNERE STADT, THE HEART OF VIENNA

44 top The ornamental motifs formed by the roof tiles of St. Stephen's Cathedral include a double-headed eagle, the symbol of the two kingdoms of Austria and Hungary.

Protected to the north by the Danube Canal and surrounded by the Ringstrasse, the Innere Stadt is the heart of the ancient and glorious city of Vienna, a maze of narrow medieval streets through which glittering monumental boulevards were cut during the 19th century. A triumph of pinnacles, spires, sculpture and decoration, the cathedral's south tower is a natural landmark visible all over the city. The Steffl, as the locals affectionately call it, is 448 ft (136 m) tall and stands on the right of St Stephen's Cathedral, the emblem of Austrian Gothic and the undisputed symbol of the city. This majestic building, 351 ft (107 m)

long and up to 112,2 ft (32,4 m) wide, took 800 years to build. "This place recounts our history: every generation has made its contribution, each in its own language," the architect-designer Adolf Loos wrote. Visitors are still greeted by the Romanesque façade erected by Ottakar II, sandwiched between the two square Roman towers and adorned with 13th-century sculpture, including the Riesentor (Giant's Door). From the first stone laid by Rudolf IV in 1359, the Steffl was built in 70 years. The 15th-century north tower was planned as its twin, but its construction was halted at a height of just 223 ft (68 m) and the tower was hastily topped with a temporary cap in the 16th century. However, the uncompleted structure has the honor of housing the Pummerin, a 22-ton bronze bell made by melting down the cannons captured from the Turks in 1683.

In 1945 the bell crashed onto the nave floor, and was recast and replaced in the tower with a solemn ceremony in 1957, marking the rebirth of the cathedral following the disastrous fire that damaged it during the World War II, and with it the whole of Vienna. The 15th-century reliefs by Hanns Puchsbaum on the Singers' Door, the "Christ with a toothache" behind the apse (an Ecce Homo whose nickname is derived from its particular facial expression) and the pulpit dating from 1430, from which St John of Capistrano preached the Crusade against the Turks (1451), are merely the best-known of the many Gothic sculptural groups – almost all original – that make the outside of the building an open-air museum. However, the cathedral's most distinctive feature is its Alpine-style pitched roof with enameled tiles that form brightly colored geometric patterns.

44 bottom
St. Stephen's Cathedral is the pulsating heart of Vienna and has become one of the city's main attractions since its construction between the 12th and 16th centuries.

45 Miraculously, the cathedral withstood two Turkish sieges and Napoleon's cannons, in addition to American bombs and Russian artillery during the final stages of World War II.

46 top left On the left side of the cathedral, its skilled architect Anton Pilgram, is shown in a relief with the tools of his trade: the compass and the square.

46 top right Saint Sebastian and Christ holding the Gospel are depicted on two finely sculpted columns in the cathedral.

46-47 The imposing vault, supported by richly decorated columns, gives the interior of the cathedral a touch of austere grandeur. The Baroque high altar was carved in marble in 1641 and its painted altarpiece shows the Martyrdom of Saint Stephan, the cathedral's patron saint. The red marble tomb of Emperor Frederick III is situated next to the altar.

Inside the building, the three naves, supported by bundle piers that continue to form the complex ribbing of the vaults, are brimming with sculptures in International Gothic style, Late Baroque paintings and altars, and objects of popular devotion. One of the highlights of the cathedral, and alone worth the trip, is the pulpit that stands against the third pier on the left, next to the delicate statue of the Virgin Mary (1325). This masterpiece was long attributed to Anton Pilgram, but today Nikolaus Gerhaert von Leyden is believed more likely to have been the carver. It is adorned with figures of the four Fathers of the Church and a portrait of the sculptor himself, peering out of a window beneath the elaborate stairs, almost as though keeping an eye on his work.

The side apses also boast important works of art: the right one houses the red marble tomb of Frederick III, which was commenced in 1467 by von Leyden, while the left one has a mighty wooden altar, carved and painted in 1447 and donated to the cathedral by the same emperor.

Around 30 years ago excavations beneath the Stephansplatz for the underground railway revealed the remains of the *Virgilkapelle* (St Virgil's Chapel), which belonged to a sacred citadel used as a cemetery that developed around the cathedral during the 13th century. The network of underground burial chambers beneath the apse (the catacombs accessible from the left transept) has been extended over the centuries and was used as an air-raid shelter during World War II.

47 The nave is dominated by a sumptuous Gothic pulpit, believed to have been carved by Nikolaus Gerhaert von Leyden in 1510, which is adorned with statues of the four Fathers of the Church, and smaller sculptures of diabolical creatures driven away by a dog. The sculptor even depicted himself looking out of a little window, known as the Fenstergucker.

48 top *The Wiener Neustädter Altar (1447) is one of the treasures housed in the cathedral. It is situated in the center of the left apse and features an altarpiece with two triptychs whose panels are painted with 72 figures of saints.*

48 bottom *The cathedral contains several tombs and was the setting for many important historical events. In 1515 it was the scene of the double marriage between the grandchildren of Maximilian I and the children of King Ladislaus II of Hungary. The funeral of Emperor Franz Joseph was also held in the cathedral, in 1916.*

48-49 *The immense array of artworks that adorns the interior of the cathedral ranges from details revealing the building's Romanesque origins to the Baroque altars.*

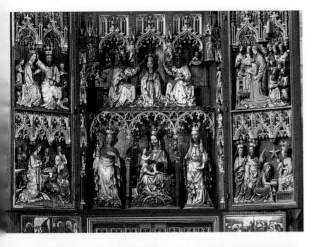

The Ducal Crypt houses several sarcophagi and about 50 urns containing the viscera of members of the Habsburg dynasty (their hearts were placed in the Augustinian Church, while their bones were housed in the Imperial Crypt in Capuchin Church). This large underground mausoleum built by Emperor Matthias (reigned 1612-1619) houses the remains of 145 members of the dynasty, including Maria Theresa and her husband in a double Rococo-style sarcophagus carved by Balthasar Ferdinand Moll, Charles VI, mourned by a touching Austria, Francis Joseph, Elizabeth and their son Rudolf.

While the Cathedral is the city's sacred emblem, the Graben, which extends where the Roman wall once stood (Graben means "trench") is as profane as can be, for it is Vienna's main shopping street, lined with handsome cafés and elegant stores. In its center, a pyramid of clouds, statues and cherubs supports a gilded copper figure of the Trinity. his is the Pestäule, a Baroque masterpiece by Johann Bernhard Fischer von Erlach, erected by Leopold I in 1693 in thanks for the end of the plague epidemic of 1679. It is framed by buildings by von Hildebrandt, Otto Wagner (who made his studio in the large glass attic of the Ankerhaus), Adolf Loos and Hans Hollein, and Biedermeier, Ringstil and Jugendstil palaces, forming an authentic anthology of civil architecture from the Baroque to the present day! The Peterskirche stands at the end of a little street leading off the northern side of the Graben. The origins of this splendid Baroque church are said to reach back to the time of Charlemagne. It was completely rebuilt in 1703-15 by Gabriel Montani and Johann Lukas von Hildebrandt, who designed the sober concave façade surmounted by a mighty oval dome adorned with stuccowork and a fresco by Johann Michael Rottmayr. The Graben meets the Kohlmarkt, the old coal merchants' street, which is now lined with prestigious stores, including the famous Demel bakery that supplied the court. Michaelerplatz, with the sumptuous entrance of the Hofburg, is just a stone's throw away. To reach the square, one passes the impressive Michaelerkirche, the former parish church of the imperial court, which houses the tomb of Pietro Metastasio, on the left, and the simple lines of the Looshaus on the right. The latter was known as the "building without eyebrows," because of the lack of ornamentation above its windows, and was so disliked by Francis Joseph that he ordered his driver to avoid Michaelerplatz whenever he arrived at or left the Hofburg!

51 top right A lead figure of Saint Joseph and Child by Johann Martin Fischer (1740-1820) replaces the original statue that dominated one of the two fountains on the Graben, dating from the 17th century.

52-53 and 53 top
A detail of a caryatid
"supporting" a building
on the Graben, and a
view of the Graben
level with the
Postsparkasse (left).

53 bottom Caryatids
are also featured on
the façades of the
buildings overlooking
the Freyung square, in
the heart of the city.
Its vicinity to the

Hofburg imperial
complex made it
a popular site for
aristocrats to build
their palaces between
the 16th and 18th
centuries.

54 top left
The elegant Palais
Ferstel was designed
in Italianate style in
the mid-19th century
by the architect
Heinrich von Ferstel
to house the Austro-
Hungarian Bank.

54 top right Vienna is
a city of caryatids and
telamones, finely
sculpted in Italian
marble, which
heightened the
splendor of its
aristocratic dwellings.
This sculpture adorns
the Palais Kinsky.

54-55 The northern
side of the Freyung is
occupied by the
Schottenkloster, or
"Scottish Monastery,"
and its church, founded
in 1155. The monks
came from Ireland,
which was then known
as New Scotland.

55 Hidden behind the
Hofburg, the Minoriten-
platz is a quiet cobbled
square surrounded by
Baroque palaces. The
14th-century tower of
the Minoritenkirche rises
in its center and features
Vienna's best-preserved
Gothic portal.

The solemn and monumental
Herrengasse is lined with noble palaces built
during the 18th and 19th centuries, which
now house ministries and public offices.
Walking along the side of the
old Landhaus, the scene of the tragic
uprising of 1848, brings one to the
Minoritenkirche.

Only the Cathedral rivals this grand
Gothic building, which was a favorite target
of the Turkish artillery during the second
Ottoman siege.

The church was probably built by the
Minorite friar James of Paris (1340), who
carved the main portal with its statues of
the Virgin and Saints, and was one of the
properties expropriated by Joseph II in
1784. The emperor commissioned Johann
Ferdinand Hetzendorf von Hohenberg to
build the current high altar and to replace
most of the furnishings.

The Freyung, a triangular medieval
square adorned with von Hildebrandt's
Palais Kinsky, can be reached through the
arcade of the Palais Ferstel, which is home
to the historic Café Central.

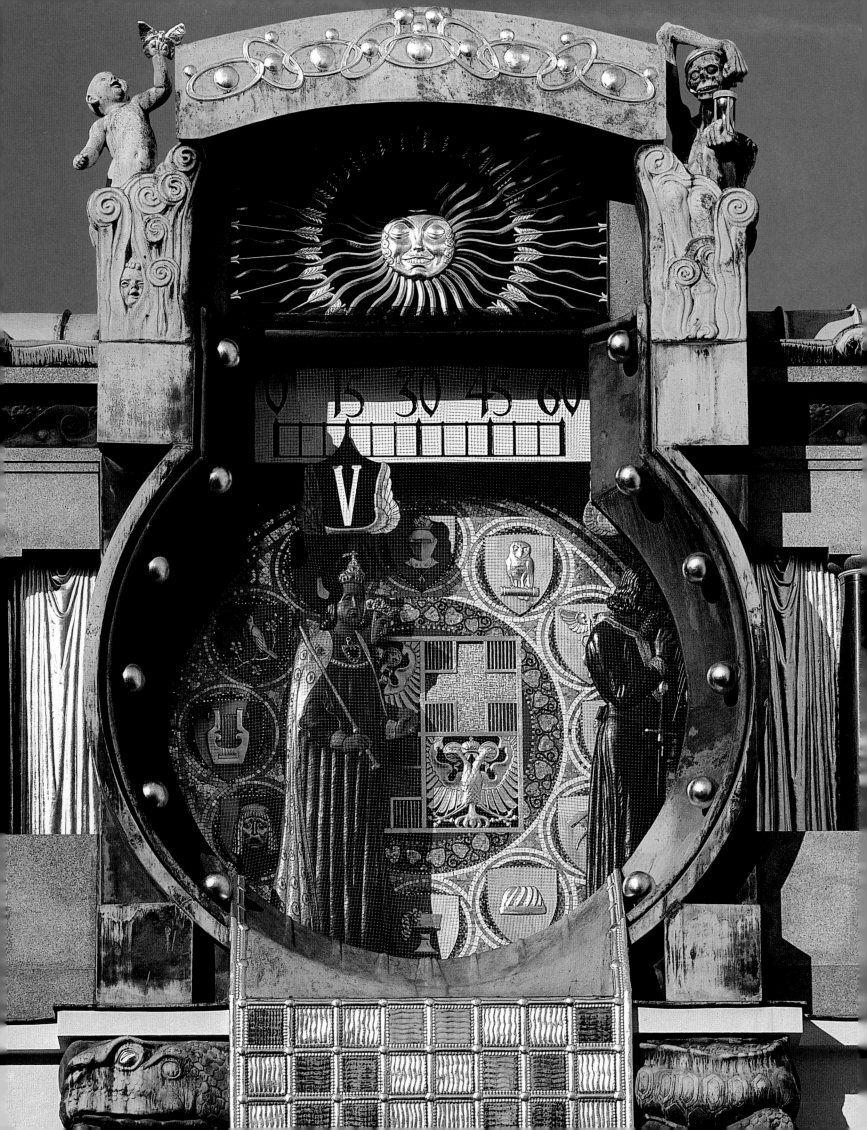

56 The Ankeruhr ("Anchor Clock"), designed by Franz von Matsch in 1914, stands on the north side of the Hoher Markt. Every hour, figures from the city's history move across the dial.

57 top left Ruprechtskirche stands in Ruprechtsplatz. The church was founded in the 8th century, although the current massive unadorned building dates from the 12th century.

57 top right Statues by Lorenzo Mattielli adorn the façade of the Arsenal (Armory), which is now the headquarters of the city fire brigade.

57 center Judenplatz is the site of the bunker-like form of the Holocaust Memorial, inaugurated in 2000.

57 bottom Once the site of public executions, the Freyung is now home to a small market.

Returning towards the Graben, one encounters another large square, which was the scene of many medieval tournaments. This is the Am Hof, the site chosen by the Babenbergs for their castle, and that of the Kirche am Hof, which developed from the Romanesque ducal chapel from the late 14th century.

The façade with its great central window overlooks the fire station, which occupies the entire opposite side of the square.

The narrow street that runs along the right side of the formal arsenal, on the far side of the square, leads to the Judenplatz, which was once the center of the old ghetto. Behind it stands the old Rathaus, whose courtyard is adorned with Raphael Donner's delightful Andromeda Fountain (1741). The city's oldest buildings are situated beyond the Wipplingerstrasse, in an area covering just a few hundred square feet: the 14th-century Maria am Gestade church, with its tall, narrow façade and seven-storied polygonal bell tower, and the Ruprechtskirche, a little jewel with a Romanesque bell tower featuring double-lancet windows.

This is the oldest church in Vienna and was built in the 11th century in a district backing onto the Danube Canal with such an intricate maze of streets as to have earned itself the nickname of "Bermuda Triangle."

It lies in the northernmost sector of the Innere Stadt, which was historically associated with the river wharfs that were replaced by Otto Wagner's Franz-Josefs-Kai, and was far removed from the control of the Hofburg.

THE RING:
A MIRACLE OF ECLECTICISM

Every cloud has a silver lining, and Napoleon, who drained the coffers of the Austrian court when he took up residence in the Schönbrunn Palace during the 1809 occupation, unwittingly did the Viennese a great favor. Indeed, as he withdrew from the city, he demolished part of the bastions that defended the Innere Stadt (obviously not very effectively).

This time, however, nobody rushed to repair the destruction. Instead, the rubble was removed and replaced by two parks – the Volksgarten for the people and the Burggarten for the court, on the west and east sides of the Hofburg respectively – and a gate, the Burgtor, was finally built to link the severely overcrowded inner city with the suburbs that had developed around it.

The entire enclosure was cleared by the

soldiers and transformed into a promenade.

At this stage the city just had to wait for a "brave" emperor to do what nobody had dreamed of doing for centuries and order the removal of the walls.

Whether to compete in grandeur with Paris, which Haussmann was adorning with grand boulevards during this period, or to make it easier to combat the new "enemy," which was no longer an outsider but was hidden within the city itself (the bastions had obstructed the imperial forces when they had attempted to suppress the uprisings in 1848), Francis Joseph gave the long-awaited order in December 1857. On January 30, 1858 a competition was announced for the rebuilding of the area.

It was one of the most prestigious commissions of the day and attracted an amazing 509 entries. However, only 85 of these actually drew up and submitted plans, from which 3 winners were chosen in the October of the same year: Eduard van der Nüll with August von Sicardsburg, Ludwig Förster and Friedrich Stache. In the event, none of these designs were built, but instead a mixture of the three was adopted to satisfy the wishes of the emperor, who continued to move the buildings on the planners' maps right through to the end of the work.

The architects gave free rein to their imagination, designing buildings inspired by the most diverse styles, from classical Greek to Renaissance, Neoclassical and Baroque, thus creating a new one that became known as Viennese Historicism.

58 The formal French garden of the Volksgarten was opened in 1820 and was once a favorite spot of the aristocracy. The northeastern corner is home to a seated statue of the Empress Elisabeth, while a monument to the poet and dramatist Franz Grillparzer stands in the opposite corner.

59 The English-style Burggarten was the private garden of the Habsburg family until 1918. It is hidden behind the Neue Burg and its entrance is adorned with the Mozart Denkmal, a marble plinth by Viktor Tilgner. It depicts somersaulting cherubs, two reliefs of Don Giovanni and portraits of Mozart's father and sister.

60 top left The University is one of the public buildings overlooking the Rathausplatz. In 1873 Heinrich Ferstel was engaged to design the faculties of Law and Philosophy, while Gustav Klimt and Franz von Matsch were commissioned to paint three murals on the walls of the great hall in 1894.

60 bottom left and right The Votivkirche, near the University (shown here, a detail of its decoration and a night view), was consecrated in 1879.

61 The nave of the Votivkirche, the monumental church built by the Viennese architect Heinrich Ferstel. It was completed in 1854 and was the first public building to appear on the Ringstrasse, before the emperor ordered the demolition of the city's fortifications.

This exasperated eclecticism (now known as Ringstil) was disparaged by many – first and foremost Adolf Loos and Otto Wagner – who considered it the product of the self-congratulatory cravings of the middle class, who built their temples here and vied with each other to obtain an apartment. With its imposing buildings and parks, the 2.5-mile (4-km) long Ringstrasse is a veritable compendium of art history. Starting at the Schottenring at its western end, the Börse (Stock Exchange), built in eclectic style in 1877 by the Danish architect Theophil Hansen, is followed by the University on the right. Founded in Iganz Seipel Square in 1365, it was later moved to this Neo-Renaissance-style building erected in by Heinrich von Ferstel (1873-83).

The Votivkirche is set back from the road, in the adjoining Rooseveltplatz. It was commissioned by Francis Joseph in 1854 on the site of the assassination attempt of 1853 and was inaugurated in 1879. It was designed by Heinrich von Ferstel, in Neo-Gothic style after the cathedrals of 13th-century France, as testified by the 325-ft (99 km) twin towers that frame its façade.

63 top The sumptuous interior of the Burgtheater is not the original one, because the theater was forced to close less than ten years after its inauguration, due to the terrible acoustics, and to replace the seats, from which the stage could not be seen.

63 center The Neue Rathaus is characterized by a central tower, approximately 325 feet tall, which is topped by the statue of an knight in armor.

63 bottom Another prominent building on Rathausplatz is the prestigious Burgtheater, which has an unfortunate history: rebuilt in 1897, it had to be reconstructed a second time after being bombed in 1945.

A little further on, separated by the Rathauspark – laid out between 1872 and 1875, and planted with majestic trees and adorned with fountains and statues – stands the Baroque-style Burgtheater (1874-88), designed by the prolific architects Gottfried Semper and Karl Freiherr von Hasenauer, and Friedrich von Schmidt's huge Neo-Gothic Rathaus (1872-83). The theater was restored after World War II and bears witness to a glorious past that produced dozens of famous actors. It boasts an elegant red, gold and ivory interior and frescoes by Gustav Klimt. The very dimensions of the Rathaus' façade (499 x 417 ft/152 by 127 m), inspired by the Town Hall in Brussels, suggest that it was built to compete with the sumptuousness of Vienna's imperial buildings. It is surmounted by four pinnacles and a central tower, topped with a metal statue of a standard-bearer. The interior is equally grand, with a huge courtyard and a Banquet Hall covering an area of 280,000 sq. ft (26,012 sq. m), while the Audience Hall has an enormous bronze chandelier weighing over 7055 lbs (3200 kg) and dating from 1873.

62 The richly decorated Gothic-Revival-style Neue Rathaus is home to Vienna's mayor and city council. The building was completed in 1883, following 11 years of work, and replaced the Altes Rathaus ("Old Town Hall"). The illustration shows the series of pointed windows that runs along the façade, above the handsome portico at street level.

64 top It is clear at a glimpse that Theophil Hansen's inspiration for the Parliament building was the architecture of classical Greece, which he considered the home of democracy.

64 bottom The Parliament building is characterized by a colonnade supported by caryatids, like the Erechtheum of the Acropolis in Athens, while its terrace is adorned with statues, reliefs and four bronze quadrigae.

64-65 In front of the Parliament building stands a huge statue of Athena, the goddess of wisdom, with a golden feather, which dominates a fountain featuring four Tritons representing the Danube, Inn, Elba and Moldova Rivers.

The peak of celebratory monumentality, however, is represented by Theophil Hansen's nearby Parliament building (1873-83), which stands opposite the Volksgarten. The building is modeled on the architecture of ancient Greece, the home of democracy.

The white marble Athena Fountain, depicts the goddess Athena with a gilded helmet and spear, surrounded by allegories of the Virtues and the Great Rivers of the Empire (carved by Kundmann in 1902), and stands in front of a double flight of stairs leading to the main entrance of the building, designed in the form of a temple with a pronaos and pediment.

The twin wings, lined with half-columns, end in temple-shaped pavilions, while the attic is topped with 60 statues of figures from Greek and Roman antiquity.

65 top left The legislative powers of the state are represented by female statues, again in classical style, at the base of the pillar supporting Athena.

65 top right The executive powers are depicted on the opposite side of the base. The fountain was built between 1893 and 1902.

66-67 The statues of the Danube and Inn Rivers in a detail of the Athena Fountain, which stands in front of the Parliament building. The structure is the work of various sculptors, carefully coordinated by Hansen.

68 top Maria-Theresien-Platz is adorned with a monumental statue of Empress Maria Theresa, surrounded by four of her generals on horseback, her physician (on foot) and three of her counselors.

68 bottom Maria-Theresien-Platz is home to one of the leading centers of culture in Vienna and the world: the Kunsthistorisches Museum, which was completed in 1891 at the same time as the square.

68-69 Maria-Theresien-Platz is particularly spectacular from above, for only a bird's-eye view allows a full appreciation of the balance created by the symmetry of the two identical buildings that house the Kunsthistorisches Museum and the Naturhistorisches Museum.

The central section of the Ringstrasse, known as the Burgring, is the province of the imperial palaces. The Hofburg stands on the left, between the Volksgarten and the Burggarten. The Volksgarten has retained its original Italian-style garden laid out in 1823, the semicircular café where the masters of the waltz once performed, and the Temple of Theseus, stripped of its statue by Canova, which has been moved to the Kunsthistorisches Museum. A little further on lies the Burggarten, which became a public park in 1919. Its leafy walks are lined with planes, chestnuts and maples, and it is easy to understand why the emperor loved to stroll around this little kingdom.

On the right of the road, the symmetrical buildings of the Naturhistorisches and Kunsthistorisches Museums stand each side of Maria-Theresien-Platz, which is dominated by a huge bronze statue of the empress on her throne (1888). They were built in Neo-Renaissance style by Semper and Hasenauer in 1872-81 and each is topped with a dome.

69 top left One of the statues of the horsemen of the Maria Theresa monument in Maria-Theresien-Platz seems to be pointing to the sandstone façade of the Kunsthistorisches Museum, commissioned by the Habsburg Emperor Franz Joseph I of Austria-Hungary.

69 top right
Completed in 1913,
when it was
inconceivable that
the era of the Austro-
Hungarian Empire
could be almost over,
the Neue Burg ("New
Palace") was the last
addition to the Hofburg
complex.
It was from a balcony
of this building that
Adolf Hitler proclaimed
the Anschluss in 1938.

70 top Originally built to house the Habsburg collections of art and curiosities, today the Kunsthistorisches Museum boasts works by Arcimboldo, Bronzino, Canova, Caravaggio, Dürer, Klimt, Raphael, Rubens, Steen, Tintoretto, Van Eyck, Velázquez and Vermeer.

70-71 An excellent example of the rich collection housed in the Kunsthistorisches Museum is Antonio Canova's marble group of Theseus and the Centaur (1812). The work is set in an ideal position, allowing the frenzied action depicted by the sculptor to overwhelm visitors ascending the stairs.

The Kunsthistorisches Museum was inaugurated in 1891 and its decorators included Ernst and Gustav Klimt. It is home to one of the world's greatest collections of 15th-to-18th-century painting, which was amassed by the enthusiastic patronage of the Habsburg family. All the great masters are represented – Titian, Tintoretto, Raphael, Veronese, Caravaggio, Giorgione, Correggio, Velázquez, Bruegel the Elder, Rubens, Rembrandt, Van Dyck, Dürer – forming an endless series of masterpieces.

While the Kunsthistorisches Museum has become an institution, it now has a competitor in the form of the Museum Quartier, inaugurated in 2001. This is one of the largest cultural complexes in the world, covering an area of 650,000 sq. ft (60,386 sq. m). It is housed in the imperial mews commissioned by Charles VI from Johann Bernhard Fischer von Erlach, whose immense 18th-century façade overlooks the square named after Maria Theresa. The Museums Quartier features design, film, e-music, fashion and new media laboratories and web cafés. Two "cubes" designed by the brothers Laurids and Manfred Ortner stand in the inner courtyard, next to the central pavilion of the new Kunsthalle Wien. The one on the left, built from Danube limestone, is the Leopold Museum, which boasts the world's largest collection of works by Egon Schiele, as well as pieces by the leading artists of the Modernist movement. The volcanic rock of the cube on the right houses the MUMOK Foundation Ludwig, Austria's foremost museum of modern and contemporary art.

71 top and center Visitors can relax, read or enjoy a cup of coffee in the huge spaces of the MuseumsQuartier. The company that manages the institution also offers scholarships to emerging artists, enabling them to spend six months at the complex. This huge cultural space – one of the ten largest in the world – also features several sections in which children can experiment and develop their creative skills with games and colors.

71 bottom The transition from imperial stables to top-level museum complex can be seen in the interiors of the MuseumsQuartier, which are a blend of classic and modern, creating rational yet traditional spaces.

72 top and center left The Danube Canal (Donaukanal), dividing the island district of Brigittenau and Leopoldstadt from the old city, is actually the narrowest of the four arms of the Danube River, which was the first to be regulated in 1598, due to its proximity to the city. Extensive work was carried out along its banks following the disastrous flooding of the Danube between 1870 and 1875. The work was performed with the use of steam engines that had been used for the excavation of the Suez Canal, while another bed was dug on the eastern side during the 1970s.

The next section of the Ringstrasse is known as the Opernring, and is home to the Neo-Renaissance building of the Vienna State Opera. It is followed by the Schubertring and the Parkring, with the Stadtpark on the right. Built in the style of an English garden in 1862 to the design of Josef Selleny and Rudolph Siebeck, the Stadtpark is the largest of the Ringstrasse's parks and covers an area of 16 acres (6.4 hectares).

The entire length of the park is crossed by the Wienfluss (Vienna River) – the only stretch that has been allowed to flow above ground – before it joins the nearby Danube Canal. The point in which the river emerges from the ground is marked by the Wienfluss-Portal (1903-07), a pure Jugendstil monument by Friedrich Ohmann and Josef Hackhofer. It is counterpointed by a neighboring spa pavilion known as the Kursalon, which was built on the side of the Parkring.

This classicizing building was erected during the 18th century and was once used for concerts.

A stroll among lakes dotted with swans and gardens allows the visitor to reach the Otto Wagner Station.

The Museum of Applied Art (MAK) stands on the corner between the Stubenring and the Weiskirchnerstrasse. It is one of the most important of its kind in Europe, and boasts a fine collection of rugs, porcelain, fabrics and enamels, but also the armchairs designed by Otto Wagner for one of his masterpieces, the nearby Austrian Postal Savings Bank building (1904-06), which emphasize the architect's functionalist style. This regular polygonal building is unadorned and features a two-story base clad with slabs of granite, which supports four marble-faced stories studded with metal rivets. It is topped with an attic and an aluminum balustrade adorned with Winged Victories by Othmar Schimkowitz. Nearby is the Danube Canal, overlooked by the Urania observatory designed by Max Fabiani. In 1910, it was the first astronomical observatory in Europe to be open to the public.

72 bottom left and top right The bed excavated during the 1970s created a new course for the river, which thus became known as the Neue Donau ("New Danube"). An artificial island was created between it and the Alte Donau ("Old Danube"), which has been transformed into a beach that attracts many locals in spring and summer. Innere Stadt aside, the Danube is the true pearl of the city, as demonstrated by these photographs: the proverbial beauty of the Blue Danube celebrated by Strauss is reflected in Vienna's handsome architecture, offering unexpected leisure spots for a large city.

73 A stone archway, adorned with reliefs of alluring naiads, frames the statue of Johann Sebastian Strauss – the "king of the waltz" – depicted playing the violin in the Stadtpark, the largest of the Ringstrasse's parks. The sculpture was carved by Edmund Hellmer in 1925.

JOHANN
STRAUSS

IMPERIAL JEWELS

HOFBURG, THE "FIRST HOME" OF THE HABSBURGS

75 top right Founded in 1768 by Duke Albert of Saxe-Teschen, the Albertina is home to one of the world's greatest collections of graphic art, featuring 50,000 drawings, engravings and watercolors and 1.5 million prints. This huge collection allows the museum to mount temporary exhibitions on different themes.

74 The Österreichische Nationalbibliothek (Austrian National Library) is the largest library in Austria and is housed in the Hofburg. The Baroque Prunksaal boasts over 200,000 volumes, papyri, globes and maps. The main reading room is open to the public.

74-75 The Heldenplatz, northwest of the Hofburg, lies in front of the curved façade of the Neue Burg. The Neoclassical Burgtor, erected to celebrate the victory over Napoleon at the Battle of Leipzig, is visible in the center of the photograph.

75 top left The Josefsplatz is one of Vienna's most imposing squares and is surrounded on three sides by the white buildings of the Hofburg. It was originally the church square of the Augustinerkirche and was subsequently used by the Spanish Riding School.

The Hofburg, in the heart Vienna, is synonymous with Habsburg power and its history spans a period of 600 years. From the 13th century to 1913 the emperors built and remodeled their palace, making it an intricate, asymmetric and stylistically diverse complex of 18 wings and 19 courtyards. It is a city within the city, with churches, chapels, museums, infinite collections of books and one of the world's largest archives of graphic art, the Albertina, which was reopened to the public in March 2003 following eight years of refurbishing and modernization.

The Bohemian king Ottakar II commenced the construction of the original castle, and other buildings developed around it during his 20-year stay in the city. The Alte Burg, renamed the Schweizertrakt (Swiss Wing) in the 18th century after the Swiss Guards who served there, became the center of this huge complex that covers an area of 2.6 million sq. ft (241-547 sq. m) and which has almost 2,600 rooms. The freestanding Stallburg and Amalienburg residences were built during

the 16th century and were connected to the Alte Burg in the following century by the Leopoldinischer Trakt (Leopoldine Wing). During the 18th century Charles VI commissioned Joseph Emanuel Fischer von Erlach to connect the remaining separate buildings. The architect created imposing Baroque palaces: on one side the Stallburg was joined to the 14th-century Augustinerkirche and the Albertina with the Austrian National Library and the Redoutensäle, and on the other to the Amalienburg with the Winter Riding School and the Imperial Chancellery Wing.

Further important work was carried out at the turn of the 20th century, with the construction of the Neue Burg on the Ring side (which, according to Gottfried Semper and Karl Hasenauer's plans, should have been faced by a twin palace that was never built owing to the outbreak of World War I) and the completion of the sumptuous entrance on Michaelerplatz in 1913 by Ferdinand Fischer, built to the 18th-century design of Charles VI's architect.

76 top The monumental Michaelertor (St. Michael's Gate) was the main entrance to the huge Hofburg Imperial Palace complex during the period of Habsburg rule and is topped with an elegant dome and Neoclassical statues.

76 bottom Situated in the southwestern corner of the Innere Stadt, the Hofburg complex – seen here from the Michaelertrakt (St Michael Wing) – spans seven centuries of architecture and bears the personal mark left by each Habsburg ruler.

77 Given the unique nature of its architecture, the Michaelertor is perhaps one of the most impressive structures of the Hofburg complex, and testifies to the power of the Austro-Hungarian Empire at its height, which was destined to last little more than 100 years after the end of the Napoleonic Wars.

78 top One of the sumptuous rooms inhabited by the Habsburg rulers. The elegant imperial apartments were decorated with tapestries, candelabras, precious fabrics, mirrors and fine furniture.

78 bottom Precious chandeliers light the Imperial Dining Room in the Hofburg, where the table is laid with silver cutlery and crystal glasses, as it was during the time of the Emperor Franz Joseph and the Empress Elisabeth.

78-79 and 79 top The Hofburg is an austere and harmonious complex both inside and out, which still betrays its past role as one of the most important centers of power in Europe. During the 16th century it was the heart of the largest empire in the world, as

Charles V himself described it. The figures are eloquent: the complex includes 18 wings, 54 staircases, 19 courtyards and 2600 rooms, which were the home of the Habsburgs for almost 700 years, from the 13th century to 1918.

A monumental staircase leads to the imperial apartments, housed in the Reichskanzleitrakt (Chancellery Wing) and the Amalienburg. The Chancellery Wing housed the offices of the Holy Roman Empire until its dissolution by Napoleon in 1806. During the mid-19th century Emperor Francis Joseph chose it for his private apartments and study, where he spent much of his time. It was here that he received the news of the suicide of Rudolf, his only son, on January 30, 1889. And it was here that he granted his daily audiences to his subjects who came to present themselves to the emperor before taking public office, convey their gratitude at receiving a military or civilian decoration, or beg for clemency for themselves or their relatives. They awaited the emperor in the Waiting Room of the Audience Chamber, dressed in uniform, tailcoat or national costume as required by court etiquette.

The rooms of Empress Elizabeth (Sisi) were in the Amalienburg, which had been the dower residence of the Empress Wilhelmine Amalia, following the death of her husband, Emperor Joseph I. Elisabeth was regarded as very beautiful and was conscious of her good looks. In order to preserve them and keep her body slim and supple, she fitted out an exercise room with wall bars and rings. However, her true realm was her dressing room, for the care of her thick, ankle-length hair required many hours each day, which she occupied by reading and listening to the recital of the verses of her favorite poet, Heinrich Heine (1797-1856) , who was depicted in four portraits on the walls.

This part of the palace also houses the Great Hall, adorned with a statue of Elisa Bonaparte by Canova; the Small Hall, where the dress that Sisi was wearing when she was assassinated in Geneva in 1898, is displayed; the Rococo apartment in which Czar Alexander I stayed during the Congress of Vienna and which was subsequently occupied by the last emperor, Charles I; and the Dining Room, with the table set as it was during the time of Francis Joseph.

The early-Baroque-style Leopoldinischer Trakt housed the private apartments of Empress Maria Theresa, which were converted to state rooms following her death in 1780. It is now houses the office of the president of the Republic of Austria. The Amalienburg also houses the Imperial Silver Collection, which features unique pieces by the most renowned European silversmiths, making it the most tangible testimony of the opulence and tastes of the Habsburg dynasty. The highlight of the collection is the Grand Vermeil service, originally made for Napoleon and purchased by Emperor Francis I during the Congress of Vienna in 1814-15, following Napoleon's defeat at Waterloo. It was subsequently expanded until reaching 140 place settings.

81 top center
Another interesting
feature of the
sumptuous In Der
Burg Square is the
clock and the sundial
on the Amalienburg,
which was built in the
16th century and
named after the
wife of Joseph I,
Wilhelmine Amalia,
who chose it as her
residence in the 18th
century.

81 top right The
Burgkapelle boasts an
unusual mixture of
styles. This imperial
chapel was built in
Gothic style in the mid-
15th century and was
subsequently partly
remodeled in Baroque
style. During Sunday
Mass, the crystal-clear
voices of the famous
Vienna Boys' Choir can
be heard beneath the
lancet arches.

The Swiss Court, whose gate, opened in 1522, is one of Vienna's few genuine Renaissance works, opens onto the *Schatzkammer* (Treasury), which houses the crown and insignia of the Holy Roman Empire, the Burgundian Inheritance and the Order of the Golden Fleece. On Sundays the Vienna Boys' Choir sings during the Mass celebrated in the nearby Burgkapelle (Palace Chapel), watched over by 13 wooden statues of saints. The Gothic Augustinerkirche was the setting for the sumptuous wedding of Francis Joseph and Elisabeth in 1854 and also the unorthodox marriage of Napoleon and Marie Louise in 1810, in which the Archduchess of Austria wed the Emperor of the French by proxy. The church has retained its original appearance and houses the silver urns containing hearts of the Hapsburg rulers and also the memorial to Marie Christine of Austria (1742-1798), sculpted by Antonio Canova. The Stallburg, with its handsome colonnaded courtyard was used to house the Lipizzaner horses of the Spanish Riding School, which still perform in the arena of the Winter Riding School.

80 A tower in typical
Austrian style rises
above one of the
wings of the Imperial
Apartments
(Kaiserappartements)
overlooking the In
Der Burg Square.

80-81 and 81 top left
A monument depicting
Franz Joseph I, dressed
in a toga as the last
emperor of the Holy
Roman Empire, has
stood in the In Der Burg
Square since 1846.

82 top An instructor at the Spanish Riding School, which boasts the noblest equestrian tradition in Europe, training a Lipizzaner stallion. The splendid arena in the Hofburg where the horses train and perform was designed by Joseph Emanuel Fischer von Erlach and was completed in 1735.

82-83 The capriole, in which the horse jumps into the air and kicks out with its hind legs, is one of the many airs performed by the Lipizzaners. The riders wear bicorn hats, brown tailcoats with two rows of six brass buttons, buckskin breeches and shiny high black boots.

83 The Lipizzaner stallions are much appreciated for their agility, elegance and stamina, and undergo a grueling training session each morning. In addition to the three fundamental gaits (walk, trot and canter), the horses perform various airs, such as the levade, in which the horse stands on its hind legs.

84-85 The splendid white Lipizzaner stallions of the Spanish Riding School perform in the Winter Riding School. The arena is decorated with stuccowork and surrounded by 46 columns, while chandeliers hang from the coffered ceiling.

86 top and center An exceptionally fine edition of the works by the ancient physicians Hippocrates and Galen and a precious heavenly globe are part of the rich collection of the Austrian National Library.

86 bottom Splendid frescoes by Daniel Gran decorate the sumptuous interior of the Prunksaal, the Baroque hall of the Austrian National Library, built in the Hofburg complex in 1723-26.

86-87 The Prunksaal is 262 feet long and 66 feet high. It houses over 200,000 volumes, including the 15,000 books of the collection of Prince Eugene of Savoy, and one of the largest collections of the writings of Martin Luther.

87 top The rich Baroque Prunksaal is adorned with statues, gold decorations, frescoes and columns. It was designed by Johann Bernhard Fischer von Erlach and his son Joseph Emanuel.

The Prunksaal, the hall of the former Imperial Library, is now the pride of the Austrian National Library, whose collection includes over 200,000 books, and numerous prints, manuscripts, period photographs and musical scores.

The central section of the 266-ft (81-m) long room is marked by Corinthian columns and houses the 15,000 books that belonged to Prince Eugène of Savoy. It is topped with an oval dome decorated with a fresco of its founder, Emperor Charles VI, by Daniel Gran. The last building of the complex, the Neue Burg, houses several sections of the Kunsthistorisches Museum. In front of its convex façade stands an equestrian statue of Eugène of Savoy, which seems about to break into a gallop across the huge Helderplatz and into the Volksgarten beyond.

FRANCISCVS IOSEPHVS
NOVI PALATII ALAM
EXSTRVXIT A D MCMVII

Österreichische
Nationalbibliothek

SCHÖNBRUNN, MARIA THERESA'S PALACE

92 Schönbrunn Palace is a masterpiece of stately grandeur and appears here with the Gloriette in the background and the main courtyard (known as the Ehrenhof), in the foreground.

92-93 and 93 top left Although the extensive Rococo modeling of Schönbrunn Palace commissioned by Maria Theresa in the 18th century has earned it a place among the world's finest palaces, little remains of Johann Bernhard Fischer von Erlach's original design.

93 top right An entire population of statues inhabits the gardens of Schönbrunn Palace, which were laid out in French style on the orders of Maria Theresa.

Only after Poland and Austria had definitively defeated the invading Turks at the gates of Vienna in 1683 did Schönbrunn become the splendid palace that UNESCO in 1996 acknowledged with its inscription on the World Heritage List. Its early history is of interest, In 1569 Maximilian II purchased the Katterburg estate, but for many decades the emperors used it merely as a hunting lodge. Indeed, it was while hunting in 1612 that the Emperor Matthias discovered the *schöner Brunnen* ("beautiful spring") that suggested the name Schönbrunn 30 years later to Eleonore Gonzaga, the wife of Emperor Ferdinand II (reigned 1619-37), who had made it the residence in which she spent her lively widowhood. However, the little castle in which she held her feasts and receptions was completely destroyed during the Turkish siege of Vienna in 1683.

After having broken the Turkish threat Leopold I (reigned 1657-1705) was finally able to dedicate himself to celebrating the power of his dynasty, and in 1686 made the estate over to his son and heir, Joseph. Leopold wanted a place for his son that would rival the magnificence of Versailles, and thus commissioned a design from Johann Bernhard Fischer von Erlach, whose first draft was so grand as to ridicule the French palace. However, it was deemed too sumptuous for traditional Austrian austerity, or perhaps for the dwindling imperial finances. Nevertheless, the emperor gave his approval to the second plans, which featured "only" 1440 rooms, and the central section of the palace was ready to be inhabited in the spring of 1700. However, Joseph's sudden death caused the work to be halted, until Charles VI gave the estate to his daughter Maria Theresa, who made it the center of political and court life during her reign (1740-1780), partly because she could not bear the gloom of the Hofburg.

She engaged the architect Nikolaus Pacassi, who built the audience chamber and imperial apartments in the east wing between 1744 and 1763, and the Blue Staircase, which led to the *piano nobile* of the west wing, preserving the original ceiling frescoes by Sebastiano Ricci (1702-03) with an *Allegory of the Princely Virtues* of Joseph I (reigned 1705-1711), in which an angel symbolizing the virtue of love takes the future emperor by the hand and shows him the path to follow. The Small Gallery, overlooking the garden, and the adjoining Great Gallery, 141 ft (43 m) long, opening onto the huge Parade Court, were built in the central section of the palace.

A mezzanine floor and several large buildings (including the Orangery) were gradually added as the imperial family grew in order to accommodate and provide for a court of over 1500 people.

In 1747 a theater was solemnly inaugurated in the Parade Court, where the empress distinguished herself as a talented singer. Once the outside of the building had been made symmetrical, the façades were completed and the state rooms decorated. The Great Gallery was decorated in white and gold, with crystal chandeliers and a vaulted ceiling with frescoes by Gregorio Guglielmi (depicting the territories of the Empire paying homage to Maria Theresa and Francis I).

The Small Gallery, used for children's parties and smaller banquets, was also decorated in white and gold and adorned with a Rococo triumph of mirrors, paintings and chinoiserie. Following the death of her consort in 1765, Maria Theresa dedicated the Vieux-Laque Room to his memory, decorating it with precious Chinese lacquers and fine walnut paneling.

95 top right One of the Bergl Rooms (Berglzimmer) of the imperial apartments. These four informal yet richly furnished rooms, decorated by the Bohemian artist Johann Wenzel Bergl, were commissioned by Maria Theresa and overlook the palace gardens. The walls are frescoed from floor to ceiling with exotic flowers and animals, set in trompe-l'oeil trellises.

96-97 The elegant Gobelin Room in Schönbrunn Palace is one of almost 1500 rooms in the former summer residence of the Habsburg family, immersed in the greenery west of the city center.

97 top Schönbrunn's Palace Chapel was consecrated in 1745, the year before the new palace, remodeled by Maria Theresa, was ready to be inhabited.

97 center The so-called "Marshal's Table," in the Rössel ("Stallions") Room was sumptuously set for dinners for the highest-ranking military officers and court officials. The room's name derives from the pictures that decorate the walls, namely portraits of horses from the imperial studs.

97 bottom During his occupations of Vienna, Napoleon stayed in what became known as the Napoleon Room, whose walnut paneling is hung with Gobelin tapestries depicting the Austrian army in Italy. The Empress Maria Theresa is said to have given birth to her children in this room, where Napoleon's son died in 1832, aged just 21.

Schönbrunn was so lovely that even Napoleon stayed there during his "visits" to Vienna. In the room named after him a portrait and a funerary mask commemorate the French emperor's only legitimate son, known as the King of Rome (or, by the Austrians, the Duke of Reichstadt), who died of tuberculosis in the palace, when just 21 years old.

In 1830 Francis Joseph was born in the Reiches Zimmer, in his parents' apartments, which now houses a sumptuous red velvet bed with gold embroidery made for Maria Theresa's marriage. He died in the west wing on November 21, 1916. "Franzl" chose to live in the other wing of the palace and his apartments include the Billiard Room, with a Biedermeier billiard table, the walnut-paneled Audience Chamber with red damask furnishings, the Study, and the Marital Bedroom, in which he died.

Sisi's rooms were arranged around the Salon, whose walls are adorned with charming pastel portraits of Maria Theresa's children by the artist Jean-Etienne Liotard. The Mirrors Rooms is a typical example of a state room from the reign of Maria Theresa. Either this room or the larger adjoining Rosa Room was the setting for the first concert given by the six-year-old Mozart in front of the empress and her fated daughter, the young Marie Antoinette. After his performance the boy leapt onto the enthusiastic monarch's lap, ignoring court etiquette. At the time of the Empress Elisabeth (Sisi), Marie Antoinette's room was used as a family dining room, and the table is still set with Viennese porcelain, silverware and crystal glasses.

98 top left
Schönbrunn's gardens are full of surprises, such as the Columbary, built during the second half of the 18th century. The four pavilions around the outside housed the birds during the night.

The fabulous palace gardens cover 300 acres (121 hectares) and are dotted with buildings, statues, mazes, artificial Roman ruins and fountains, set among tree-lined avenues. At the end of the 17th century Jean Trehet built a garden in French Baroque style, but the current layout of the grounds was designed by Nicolas Jadot de Ville-Issey and Adrian von Steckhoven between 1740 and 1780. Maria Theresa's husband's keen interest in natural history led him to found the Menagerie in 1751 (making it the oldest zoo in the world). It was designed by Jadot, who arranged the animal enclosures radially around a central pavilion, where the imperial couple occasionally ate breakfast.

The entire complex is crowned by the Gloriette, on top of Schönbrunn Hill. It was built by Johann Ferdinand Hetzendorf von Hohenberg in 1775 and consists of a central section (now the Café Gloriette) flanked on each side by two arcaded wings with Doric columns. Three flights of marble steps lead to the entrance, while a spiral staircase allows access to the flat roof, 65 ft (19.8 m) above the ground, which offers spectacular views. The overall effect of the building is enhanced with sculptural groups and two pools that reflect its architecture.

At the foot of the hill, marking the edge of the Great Parterre, stands the Neptune Fountain, designed by the same architect and completed in 1780.

A sculptural group by Wilhelm Beyer rises from the water. At the foot of the mighty sea god with his trident, the Tritons restrain the sea horses, while on his left the kneeling sea nymph Thetis begs him to help her son Achilles to reach Troy by sea. On his right sits a naiad with a cornucopia, symbolizing the fertility of the land fed by water.

Francis Joseph ordered the construction of the Palm House (1882), an impressive iron structure 370 ft (112 m) long consisting of a central pavilion 82 ft (25 m) high and two lateral pavilions 25 ft (7.6 m) high, linked by tunnel-like passages.

At the end of the 19th century, Schönbrunn was surrounded by open countryside. Today the city has enveloped it, making it a peaceful haven from the bustle of urban life.

THE PRINCE'S BELVEDERE

Eugène of Savoy arrived in Vienna in 1683, aged 20. Louis XIV had refused to give him a commission in the French army, prompting him to offer his services to Leopold I. He immediately distinguished himself against the Turks, achieving an amazing victory at the Battle of Zenta, and his fame reached every corner of Europe (Napoleon later described him as the greatest military genius in history).

The rest of his career seemed effortless: after having been elevated to the rank of general, he drove back the Turks from Hungary once and for all, bringing the kingdom back under Austrian rule (1699), and fought against the French king who had rejected him in the War of the Spanish Succession. He amassed a great fortune, which he used to assemble a fabulous art collection. At the beginning of the 18th century he commissioned the construction of a summer residence on a sloping plot near Karlsplatz from the architect Johann Lukas von Hildebrandt, the rival of Johann Bernhard Fischer von Erlach, who had built the Baroque winter palace near the cathedral in 1698, and was at the time engaged in the construction of Schönbrunn. In less than a decade von Hildebrandt built a palace that was so sumptuous and elegant that it overshadowed that of the emperor.

The Lower Belvedere (1714-16) was designed as a princely residence. Its two façades – one overlooking the octagonal courtyard, visible to those arriving from the city center, and the other rising above the gardens – have an identical central section crowned by balustrades adorned with statues. Inside, the double-height Marble Hall is decorated with stuccowork and a ceiling with a splendid fresco of Prince Eugène's victory over the Turks, painted by Martino Altomonte. Today it houses the Baroque Museum, with the grotesques carved by Messerschmidt, who portrayed himself pulling faces at the onlooker.

The nearby Orangery now houses the Museum of Medieval Art. A huge terraced garden, transformed by the skilled landscape architect of Versailles, Dominique Girard, into a geometric arrangement of flowerbeds and large parterres with fountains, waterfalls and mythological statuary, leads to the Upper Belvedere (1721-22).

100-101 The Lower Belvedere houses the Barockmuseum, with Baroque paintings and sculptures from the golden century of Viennese art, and the Museum Mittelalterlicher Kunst (Museum of Medieval Art).

101 top The Upper Belvedere is preceded by exotic statues of sphinxes, according to the tastes of the period, offering a touch of lightness to the complex. Eugene of Savoy was renowned not only for his military and diplomatic skills, but also as a lover of beauty.

102 top The semicircular pediment over the entrance to the Upper Belvedere is occupied by an elaborate coat of arms.

102 bottom An aerial view reveals the grandeur of the Belvedere complex, set among gardens that were laid out before the building was even finished.

102-103 The Upper Belvedere was designed by Johann Lukas von Hildebrandt, a popular architect and rival of Johann Bernhard Fischer von Erlach, who was responsible for many of the buildings constructed for the imperial family. The palace was built very rapidly between 1721 and 1722.

The monumental façade of the palace is reflected in the water of a pool, which replicates the three-arched balcony of the central section guarded by enigmatic sphinxes and horses, the octagonal pavilions at the ends of the wings, and the copper roofs that intentionally evoke the tents of the Turkish vizier, with whom its owner was well acquainted. The low ceiling of the Sala Terrena is supported by huge marble figures of Atlas. The rooms that now house a rich gallery of masterpieces stretching from the Neo-Classical period to the 20th century are adorned with stuccowork and Rococo decorations like a precious jewel.

However, Prince Eugène was not able to enjoy this marvelous abode for long, as he died a bachelor in 1736, aged 72, and his fortune passed to his niece. The complex was sold in 1752 to Maria Theresa, who gave it the name Belvedere because of its magnificent views, immortalized in a painting by Bernardo Bellotto, Canaletto's nephew. In 1896 the composer Anton Bruckner spent the last year of his life in an outbuilding of the upper palace, which was inhabited by the heir to the throne Archduke Francis Ferdinand from 1899. Following their purchase by the state, the two buildings became the setting for important historical events, such as the signing of the peace treaty that ended the Allies' occupation of Austria in 1955, and the ratification of the Constitution during the same year.

103 top left The vault of the entrance hall of the Upper Belvedere, known as the Sala Terrena, is supported by Atlases carved by Lorenzo Mattielli (1688-1748), The elegant decorations, which are particularly sumptuous at the base of the arches, were not completed until 1723, a year after the building was finished.

103 top right The dazzling white of the statues of the Upper Belvedere vies with that of the palace itself, whose façade – shown here from an unusual angle – ends in two pavilions. It is said that the form of the copper domes of these structures echoes those of the Ottoman tents, in honor of the prince's military achievements.

THE PLEASURES OF THE CAPITAL

THE TEMPLES OF MUSIC

105 top The Vienna State Opera was inaugurated in 1869 with Mozart's Don Giovanni, *and was the first building to be constructed on the Ringstrasse. Success in this opera house is considered the consecration of a singer's or a conductor's artistic career.*

104 A monumental staircase leads to the galleries of the Vienna State Opera. The building was erected between 1861 and 1869 by Eduard van der Nüll and was rebuilt by Erich Boltenstein following heavy damage suffered during World War II. It reopened on November 5, 1955 with Beethoven's Fidelio.

104-105 Even those who know nothing about opera can appreciate the grandeur of its Viennese temple, the State Opera. The current building, however, is not the original opera house, which was destroyed at the end of World War II and rebuilt following the Allied withdrawal from the city.

What do *Le Nozze di Figaro* by Mozart, *Fidelio* by Beethoven and *The Blue Danube* by Strauss have in common? The answer is easy: they were all composed in Vienna. The first in the 18th-century Figaro-Haus in Domgasse, behind the cathedral, where Mozart lived between 1784 and 1787. The second (like Beethoven's Fourth, Fifth and Sixth Symphonies) was composed in the Pasqualati-Haus between the Freyung and the university and performed for the first time on November 20, 1805 at the Neoclassical-style Theater an der Wien built by Franz Jäger (1801) just outside the old city walls. Finally, Johann Sebastian Strauss' composed his most famous waltz in his house on Praterstrasse, in the former Jewish quarter of Leopoldstadt. With his

500 waltzes, polkas, quadrilles and marches, Strauss was the undisputed king of dance music, which remains one of the great passions of the Viennese.

Haydn, Gluck, Mozart, Beethoven, Schubert, the Strauss family, von Suppé, Brahms, Léhar, Schönberg, Webern, but also Draghi, Caldara and Salieri: it is impossible to list all the places – monuments, theaters, commemorative plaques, tombs and apartments – associated with the memory of these legendary figures who lived and worked in the Austrian capital. Mozart alone changed address 13 times during his repeated stays in Vienna, while nobody can remember exactly how many different buildings were home to Beethoven between 1792 and 1827 (some say 24, others 40, and some even 80!). However, the German appears to be the most celebrated composer, with two busts, two funerary monuments, three memorials, eight memorial tablets and, of course, an unspecified number of houses.

In his *Wiener Musiker-Gedenkstätten*, the keen and obsessive professor Helmut Kretschmer is the only person to have had the courage and patience to catalog and describe in detail everything belonging to the Viennese world of music. This of course includes its institution and symbol, the Vienna State Opera, one of the most famous opera houses in the world, which dominates the Ringstrasse. It was founded as the opera house of the imperial court and was one of the first buildings to be completed on the new boulevard opened by Emperor Francis Joseph. On July 10 1860, a competition was announced for its construction. It attracted 35 entries and the

first prize was awarded to the Viennese architects August Sicard von Sicardsburg, who designed the Neo-Renaissance exterior, and Eduard van der Nüll, who designed the interiors.

On May 25, 1869, the opera house was inaugurated with Mozart's *Don Giovanni*, but unfortunately neither of its architects were present, for Nüll had committed suicide at the beginning of the previous year, crushed by the public's fierce criticism of his work, and his partner had died of a heart attack two months later. The building was bombed during World War II and restored in 1955. Two fountains by Josef Gasser stand either side of the opera house, whose façade is adorned with a portico and arcade with statues in the upper arches and the pediment. Inside, 16,000 of the total area of 97,000 sq. ft (9011 sq. m) are occupied by the stage, which is able to house up to 110 orchestra players.

The 2200 seats are arranged in three tiers of boxes, a balcony and a gallery. A magnificent staircase leads to the second-floor foyer, which is decorated with handsome watercolors by Moritz von Schwind depicting everyday scenes from the meeting places of Viennese intellectuals.

*106 The large
Karlsplatz extends
in front of the
Karlskirche. The
southern side of the
square is adorned with
handsome gardens
and a fountain
(bottom). The entire,
irregularly shaped area*

*was carved out during
the second half of the
19th century during
urban remodeling. The
dimensions of Otto
Wagner's pavilion,
visible in the
background, give an
idea of the vastness
of the square.*

*106-107 The Karlskirche
rises imposingly above
the Karlsplatz and is
reflected in a lake. The
church is dedicated to
Saint Charles Borromeo,
who was canonized for
the succor that he gave
to plague victims during
the epidemic in Milan.*

*107 top right The huge
pavilion designed by
Otto Wagner in 1898 as
the Stadtbahn railway
station now serves as
the entrance to the
subway station.*

The impressive Karlskirche, with its 236-ft (72-m) high dome, dominates Karlsplatz. Dedicated to St Charles Borromeo, archbishop of Milan and protector of plague victims, the church is a sumptuous and eclectic Baroque masterpiece. It was commissioned by Charles VI, in fulfillment of a vow that he had made to the saint who had been invoked to protect the city when it was struck by a terrible plague epidemic in 1713. The new building was given to the Order of the Knights of the Holy Cross in 1737-38, and became the patronal church of the empire in 1783. The façade, characterized by an elegant portico with a pediment decorated with a relief depicting the end of the plague and inscribed with the emperor's vow, ends in two low bell towers. It is flanked by two white triumphant columns, 108 feet tall, inspired by Trajan's Column in Rome and decorated with scenes from the life of St Charles Borromeo. The well-lit interior has an oval plan with two main chapels on the sides and four smaller ones on the diagonals. Above the high altar, with a painting depicting the ascension of the saint, is a splendid Rococo decoration. The side chapels also boast fine altarpieces, with the *Assumption of the Virgin* on the left and *Saint Elizabeth of Thuringia* on the right. Above the organ, in the choir is a fresco of *Saint Cecilia with Angel Musicians*. Finally, the garden in front of the church is home to a monument commemorating the composer Johannes Brahms.

*107 top left The
enormous Italian-style
dome of the Karlskirche,
Vienna's largest and
most imposing Baroque
church, is flanked by*

*two huge columns,
inspired by Trajan's
Column. The columns
are crowned by
enormous gilded
Habsburg eagles.*

108-109 The Karlskirche's large windows illuminate the frescoes adorning the dome and make the whole building seem light and airy.

110 top The classic terracotta exterior of the Musikverein imitates the Vienna State Opera with its front portico.

A little farther on, leaving the Kärntnerring on the right, stands the Musikverein, the city's main concert hall, which overlooks the huge Karlsplatz.

This Neo-Renaissance-style building, built by Theophil Hansen between 1867 and 1870, is the home of the Society of Friends of Music, established in 1812, and the legendary Vienna Philharmonic Orchestra, founded in 1842 by Otto Nicolai in the Palais Karl Erzherzog (where the Haus der Musik, a multimedia

music museum, was inaugurated in June 2001). In keeping with the tradition of not appointing its own permanent conductor, the orchestra has been conducted by famous figures including Gustav Mahler, Richard Strauss, Arturo Toscanini, Herbert von Karajan, Zubin Mehta, Claudio Abbado and Riccardo Muti. Each year the Vienna New Year's Concert is held in the Goldener Saal, which boasts perfect acoustics and a seating capacity of 2000, and is televised worldwide.

110-111 The heart of the Musikverein is the elegant and well-proportioned Goldener Saal. It is well worth attending a concert to appreciate the magnificent acoustics of this famous room, which fully deserves its alternative name of Grosser Saal (Great Hall).

111 The decoration of the cupolas and ceilings of the Musikverein is extremely rich, but also extraordinarily well balanced. Even those who have never visited the city are probably familiar with these interiors, as the Vienna Philharmonic Orchestra's New Year's Concert is broadcasted worldwide each year from the Musikverein.

Proceeding along Lothringer Strasse, in an anticlockwise direction, one crosses the Schwarzenbergplatz to reach the Konzerthaus, the home of the city's second orchestra, the Vienna Symphony. This building is a peculiar mixture of classical and Jugendstil architecture, built in 1912-13 by Ferdinand Fellner and Hermann Helmer. The foyer is adorned with a copy of Kaspar von Zumbusch's Beethoven Monument (1880), which stands in the nearby square named after the composer. This virtual tour of the sites associated with the great maestros ends at the Zentralfriedhof, where many Viennese and foreigners are "officially" buried. It lies a little off the beaten track, at the southeast end of Simmeringer Hauptstrasse. The central section, reserved for notables, features a

112-113 Vienna is a moving sight at night, when it offers views such as this one of the Schwarzenbergplatz, one of the city's handsomest squares, adorned with the great Hochstrahlbrunnen Fountain, inaugurated in 1873.

mixture of tombs and cenotaphs in the most diverse styles. It is the final resting place of Mozart, Beethoven, Brahms, Gluck, Schönberg, Schubert, Lanner and the Strauss family. It is the "official" burial place because the mortal remains of Mozart, for example, really lie elsewhere. The composer died in 1791, honored but in straitened circumstances, aged just 35, and was given a simple but dignified burial in a marked plot designed for six interments. Later, attempts were made to identify the specific site of his grave within the plot and to mark what was believed to be correct spot with a sculpture by Hans Gassen. This monument was subsequently transferred to the group of famous musician graves in 1891. A worker in the little St Marx cemetery marked the place where the monument had earlier stood with a small column and a cherub, which were restored in 1950.

113 A sumptuous tomb set among the greenery of the Zentralfriedhof (Central Cemetery) houses the mortal remains of Johann Strauss. Father and son distinguished themselves in Vienna as the unsurpassed masters of the waltz.

THE CAFÉS, THE HOME OF VIENNESE CULTURE

"The bells of the Michaelerkirche were striking nine when Georg stopped in front of the café. He saw the critic Rapp seated beside an uncurtained window with a pile of newspapers in front of him.

"These two lines from *Der Weg ins Freie* reveal one of Albert Schnitzler's daily habits, for Freud's "literary double" was a regular of the Café Griensteidl, on the corner between Herrengasse and Schauflergasse. It was a habit shared by Hugo von Hofmannsthal – the author of the libretti of Richard Strauss' most important operas, including *Der Rosenkavalier* and *Die Frau ohne Schatten* – who had acquired it while he was a high-school student with dreams of becoming a writer. However, this was nothing out of the ordinary in Vienna: Karl Kraus, the irreverent founder of the newspaper *Die Fackel*, penned his biting satire at a table in the Café Central, which was "discovered" by the poet Peter Altenberg, who wrote, "Being at a café is like being at home without being home." He was followed by the playwright Stefan Zweig and Robert Musil (who suffered from claustrophobia and thus sat near the entrance), both Jews who were later forced to flee the country in order to escape Nazi persecution.

The essayist Alfred Polgar, who enjoyed a nightcap in nearby Michaelerplatz, often spent his days here, because he maintained that the Central was not a café, "but a vision of the world." The café, on the ground floor of the Palais Ferstel in Herrengasse 14 – a handsome Neo-Renaissance building erected in 1856-60, which now houses stores, restaurants and offices – still has a monument to the progenitor of its illustrious clients in the

114 Vienna is not only the capital of music, but also the capital of cafés and pastry shops, and is home to famous establishments such as the Café Central. Today the city boasts 562 coffee houses, 243 pastry shops with café, and 1247 bars.

114-115 The sumptuous interior of the historic Café Central, in Herrengasse 14, is always very lively. During the 20th century its tables were frequented by the most representative figures of the Viennese cultural scene.

form of a wax statue in its elegant inner room. Like the Café Central, Vienna's other coffeehouses also had their own assiduous clients.

At the turn of the 20th century the cafés became the focus of the city's cultural life, where artists, musicians, men of letters and intellectuals gathered to pass their time alone or in company, working or reading the newspapers, playing chess or enjoying a game of billiards, a former aristocratic pastime that the coffeehouses had made popular. According to tradition, it was a Polish spy called Franciszek Jerzy Kulczycki, who stole the sacks of coffee beans from the Turks, initially believing them to be camel feed. However, it was the Armenian Johannes Diodato, a spy for the Austrians, who obtained the monopoly over the coffee trade for about 20 years before falling into disgrace for his double-dealing.

During the 18th century four of his compatriots were granted authorization to sell the exotic drink by Leopold I. Fourteen years later Vienna had eleven cafés, which rapidly multiplied, becoming the center of the city's social and cultural life.

Klimt and his Secessionist companions met at the Café Museum in Friedrichstrasse 6, which was also frequented by Albert Loos, who designed its "nihilist" décor in 1899. Other illustrious clients included Kraus, Musil, Oskar Kokoschka and Nobel prizewinner Elias Canetti, who used it to gather ideas for his *Die Blendung*. Although the mirrors and Thonet chairs have disappeared, the café still attracts the new generations of intellectuals.

116 and 117 bottom Three views with buildings in very different styles illustrate Vienna's amazing and unrivaled architectural variety. The beauty of the Austrian capital is even more impressive considering that much of what can be seen today was rebuilt after World War II, or miraculously survived the catastrophe.

116-117 The end of the 19th century was a florid period for architecture, which reflected the growing trend to draw inspiration and techniques from international sources. Shown here is the Secession building, completed in 1898.

117 top The Secession was designed by Joseph Maria Olbrich for exhibitions of the artistic movement after which it was named. Three wise owls look out from the wall on one side, while the entrance is adorned with gorgons, salamanders and gilded foliage.

118-119 The Secession is topped with a dome of gilded laurel leaves designed by Gustav Klimt. The movement's motto is carved above the entrance: "To every era its art. To art its freedom."

120 top left The interior of the famous Café Sacher in the historic hotel of the same name. Here clients can enjoy a Viennese culinary legend: the delicious Sachertorte invented by the 16-year-old Franz Sacher in 1832, which has become one of the most popular cakes in the world.

120 top right Horse-drawn carriages in Albertinaplatz offer tours of the city, taking in Vienna's most important monuments, buildings and institutions. The white monument is a memorial by Alfred Hrdlicka that commemorates the atrocities of World War II.

120-121 A carriage passing the Café Mozart in Albertinaplatz 4. The sumptuous interior is decorated with wooden paneling and crystal chandeliers. Vienna is the capital of cafés, and boasts hundreds of historic establishments that continue to draw locals and tourists alike.

Each morning Thomas Bernhard (1931-89) took his contrasting sentiments of love and hate for the city and its inhabitants to the austere Café Bräunerhof in Stallburgasse 2, where he sat alone ("better the purgatory of solitude than the hell of company") to devour mountains of newspapers. Like Arik Brauer and Ernst Fuchs, the visionary environmentalist architect and painter Friedensreich Hundertwasser frequented the Café Hawelka in Dorotheergasse 6, a stone's throw from the Graben. This coffeehouse has changed little since 1910, its smoky rooms papered with yellowing posters and leaflets, where customers can enjoy delicious pastries with vanilla sauce. The only historic coffeehouses of the Ringstrasse to have survived are the Café Landtmann opposite the Burgtheater (favored by Joseph Roth and today a gathering place for Viennese theatrical performers) and the Café Schwarzenberg in Kärntnerring 17. The two rival establishments that claim to hold the original recipe for Sachertorte, the delicious chocolate cake with apricot jam, also deserve a mention. The first is the Café Demel (Kohlmarkt 14), which is richly furnished with mirrors and velvet. It was founded in 1776 by a German, whose son gave it to his talented assistant Christof Demel. Today it continues to bake cakes and pastries like those supplied to the imperial court. Its rival is the café of the Hotel Sacher (Philharmonikerstrasse 4), the refuge of the hungry guests of Francis Josef.

121 The elegant and opulent interior of the former court bakery Demel, in Kohlmarkt 14, exudes an atmosphere of bygone times. Founded in 1888, the establishment supplied its cakes to the imperial court.

THE CITY OF PARKS

122 top The figure of Bacchus stands on a building in the suburb of Grinzing, proclaiming the area's winemaking vocation. The district is famous for its Heurigen, taverns that serve the locally produced new wine.

122-123 The red roofs and gray asphalt are dominated by lush greenery in Grinzing. Great attention is paid to the conservation of both culture and nature in this area.

123 top left Apart from the colors, which are perhaps brighter than in the past, time seems to have stood still in Grinzing, where one almost expects to stumble across Mozart seeking inspiration in one of the many Heurigen.

123 top right It is said that there are more taverns than houses in Grinzing, and the reason seems clear: the rustic air of the district is a panacea for those wishing to escape the frenzied pace of the city.

123 center right and bottom right Handsome buildings characterize Grinzing, in the 19th district of Vienna. Here, the old houses and narrow streets are set among gardens and vineyards. The Heurigen are an old

Viennese institution, which were traditionally marked by a couple of conifer or fir twigs hung above the entrance. While there are many in the city proper, the majority are situated in the suburbs, e.g. Nussdorf and Sievering.

The figures leave no doubt: Vienna is one of the greenest cities in Europe, with approximately 77 of the 95 sq. miles (199 of the 246 sq. km) of its metropolitan area covered with parks, gardens and woods. Indeed, the west side of the city is surrounded by the Wienerwald (Vienna Woods), saved from clearance in the 19th century by Josef Schöffel, an early environmentalist. The Austrian capital is also proud of its status as the only wine-producing capital in Europe, with 1730 acres (700 hectares) of vineyards. This too is an ancient tradition, for the Romans were already cultivating vines on this stretch of the Danube in the 3rd century AD. Nestling among the vineyards that cover the hills surrounding the capital, the "wine" village of Grinzing is well worth a visit. Although it is actually included in Vienna's 19th district, it has preserved its atmosphere of a fairytale village. Its narrow streets are lined with little old houses, never more than two stories high, painted in delicate pastel hues. A stroll around the village reveals its Heurigen, rustic taverns with a convivial atmosphere, which serve the potent, new wine drunk immediately after the vintage, known as Heurige (from *heurig*, meaning "this year's").

These locales have become a Viennese institution and are favorite haunts of the city's inhabitants, who gather to drink wine accompanied by cured meats and cheeses and to listen to traditional live music, particularly on autumn weekends.

The KunstHausWien (Weissgerberstrasse 13) houses a permanent collection of the work of the painter Friedensreich Hundertwasser (1928-2002) and temporary exhibitions of contemporary art. The building has several stories and is characterized by irregular glass, metal, brick and wood elements.

Formerly the bentwood Thonet furniture factory, Hundertwasser bought the edifice and remodeled it in his own particular style before opening it in 1991. Nearby is the so-called "Hundertwasserhaus," Vienna's most original public housing complex. Its unusual and colorful architecture makes it stand out from the classical buildings surrounding it.

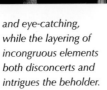

124 top The Hundertwasserhaus, built between 1977 and 1986, is a sort of personal manifesto of its architect, who used it to make one of the most important contributions to the organic architecture movement of Frank Lloyd Wright (1867-1959).

124 center and bottom The decorative technique chosen by Hundertwasser, with ceramic fragments in the mortar, is simple

and eye-catching, while the layering of incongruous elements both disconcerts and intrigues the beholder.

125 The genial artist Friedensreich Hundertwasser transferred all the facets of his nature to his works, as in the Hundertwasserhaus in Vienna: his love of freedom, both strictly and metaphorically speaking, and the release from fixed schemata and constraints.

126 Hundertwasser made his first design inspired by nature at the age of six, revealing a clear talent. However, he later expressed the idea that works such as the KunstHausWien are the houses of the artist's dreams, suggesting the fascinating idea of being able to create by transposing the oneiric sphere upon reality.

126-127 The KunstHausWien is housed in an old furniture factory and stages temporary exhibitions of contemporary artists. Two floors are dedicated to the life and art of Friedensreich Hundertwasser.

128 and 129 top
The Ferris wheel in
the Prater offers a
magnificent view of the
city, set among the
greenery and crossed
by the Danube.

129 center Seen here
from the top of the
Riesenrad, the giant
Ferris wheel, the Prater
is a huge green area of

over 4200 acres
overlooking the
Danube, with
attractions, sports
facilities and open-air
cafés and restaurants.

129 bottom Not far
from the city center,
the Prater reveals a
different Vienna, which
has abandoned its
austere imperial guise.

Then there is the Danube-Auen National Park, founded in 1996 to protect the wild and marshy environment of the stretch of river between Vienna and Bratislava, Slovakia. A small part of this exceptional habitat, essential for many animal species, lies within Vienna's municipal territory. However, the symbol of the capital's parks is undoubtedly the Wiener Prater, with its huge Ferris wheel (Riesenrad). It is reached by crossing the Canal, as this 4200-acre (1700-hectare) area of greenery lies between the Danube and the Danube Canal, occupying much of the Leopoldstadt district. The Prater was a royal hunting ground in the Middle Ages and was opened to the public in 1766 by Joseph II, who created a recreational area with swings and cafés near the Praterstern, in the far northwestern corner.

This area lies at the opposite end of the Hauptallee – the three-mile tree-lined avenue laid out by Ferdinand I in 1538 – to the little hunting lodge that Isidore Canevale transformed into the two-story pavilion known as the Lusthaus in 1784, whose interior is still adorned with frescoes of Diana, the goddess of hunting. The Volksprater was one of the first amusement parks in Europe and in 1815 already boasted dozens of wondrous attractions, along with legions of tightrope walkers, conjurers and puppeteers. The famous Ferris wheel was installed in 1897 to celebrate the golden jubilee of Francis Joseph, who commissioned it from the Englishman Walter Bassett. However, almost everything in the park was destroyed in two fires (in 1937 and 1945), including the pavilions of the 1873 Universal Exposition. Today the Prater is home to a planetarium, a soccer museum and Vienna's trade fair district, in addition, of course, to the Ferris wheel, which was rebuilt (although only 15 of the original 30 gondolas were replaced) and still allows visitors to admire views of the city from 215 ft (65 m) above the ground. Beyond the Praterstern lie the gardens of the Palais Augarten, laid out in Baroque style by Jean Trehet in 1712 and opened to the public in 1775, as commemorated by an inscription on the arch built in 1781 by Isidore Canevale. Since 1712 the Palais Augarten has housed the world's oldest porcelain factory after that of Meissen, which now features a museum and a shop; while another wing houses the boarding school of the Vienna Boys' Choir.

130 left Skyscrapers in UNO City. The modern center, whose construction commenced in 1973, assures the Austrian capital a leading role on the international scene.

130 top right UNO City employs 4000 people from 100 different countries, only a third of whom are Austrian, confirming the country's traditional cosmopolitan and constructive bent.

130-131 A view of UNO City from the Danube. The complex is formed by six Y-shaped glass office towers up to 400 feet tall, which radiate out from the central block.

131 top left A view of the modern UNO City complex, whose official name is the Vienna International Centre (VIC). In 1979 it became the third international headquarters of the United Nations, following New York and Geneva, and is home to the International Atomic Energy Agency, the United Nations Industrial Development Organization and the United Nations High Commissioner for Refugees.

131 top right Johann Staber's luminous and linear design for UNO City provoked much controversy, directed not only at the cost, which was met by taxpayers, but also on the Y-shaped plans of the buildings, considered impractical by many.

132-133 The celebrated light of the Viennese sky is reflected by a sculpture at UNO City. This gleaming international center is a promise for the future for this city whose noble history is clouded by certain dark episodes.

The next stop on our tour is the artificial island between the Danube and the Old Danube. The Donaupark, with its lawns, cycle tracks and well-equipped bathing establishments (the Viennese call the beach on the bank of the Neue Donau "Copa Cagrana," after the name of the nearby district of Kagran), was built in 1964 for the International Gardening Exhibition. It covers an area of 247 acres (100 hectares) alongside the Vienna International Centre, the United Nations complex designed by Johann Staber and inaugurated in 1979. The 827-ft (252-m) tall Donaturm rises above the six concave towers that house the International Atomic Energy Agency and the United Nations Industrial Development Organization, and has become the umpteenth symbol of Vienna.

INDEX

PHOTO CREDITS

136 The Michaelertor was the main entrance to the Hofburg Imperial Palace during the period of Habsburg rule. It is part of the Michaelertrakt wing of the complex, which was built between 1881 and 1889.